The Best
Women's Stage Monologues
of 2002

Smith and Kraus *Books for Actors*

MONOLOGUE AUDITION SERIES

YOUNG ACTOR MONOLOGUE SERIES

If you require prepublication information about upcoming Smith and Kraus books, you may receive our semiannual catalogue, free of charge, by sending your name and address to *Smith and Kraus Catalogue, PO Box 127, Lyme, NH 03768.* Or call us at *(800) 895-4331; fax (603) 643-6431.*

The Best
Women's Stage Monologues
# of 2002

edited by D. L. Lepidus

MONOLOGUE AUDITION SERIES

A SMITH AND KRAUS BOOK

Published by Smith and Kraus, Inc.
177 Lyme Road, Hanover, NH 03755
www.SmithKraus.com

© 2003 by Smith and Kraus, Inc.
All rights reserved
Manufactured in the United States of America

First Edition: October 2003
10 9 8 7 6 5 4 3 2 1

Cover illustration by Lisa Goldfinger
Cover design by Julia Hill Gignoux

The Monologue Audition Series
ISSN 1067-134X
ISBN 1-57525-327-5

Contents

Foreword

If you have bought this book, or are thinking of buying this book, most likely you are a student or aspiring professional actor always in search of monologues to work on in class or to use for auditions. Or, maybe you're a teacher, looking for exciting new material for your students. It is my firm belief that the monologues in this book will suit your needs perfectly.

For one thing, they are almost all from published, readily available plays. (See Permission Acknowledgments section in the back of this book for publisher information. If the play has not been published, though, I have included information as to how to get the complete script from the author. After all, you have to read the entire play to better understand the piece you are working on.

And here's another thing, although I have included monologues for a wide range of actors, from teens to octogenarians, the lion's share are for younger actors — teens to thirties — because that's who, by and large, needs these books the most. Which is not to say that some of the pieces for older actors aren't fabulous. They are. The two monologues from Don Nigro's *November* come to mind, or one from Bill C. Davis' *Avow*. And there are some fine pieces for those of you "of a certain age" — something for everyone from Smith and Kraus!

I have tried to give a sense of each monologue's context with my brief introductions to each piece; but, inevitably, you'll have questions. Hooray! Now you can read the whole play!

Well, kids, I'm off to being work on the 2003 monologue books. Oh boy, I can't wait — hundreds of more plays to read!

— D. L. Lepidus

ALL THINGS BEING EQUAL
Leonora B. Rianda

Comic

Helen, a writer, forty, is having a conversation with a character in her novel, whom she has just killed off.

HELEN: "Look, Ma! Top of the world!" Wow. It's so — clear from up here. Look, look! My house — there's my house! And there's the freeway I take every single goddamned morning to work for nine years! *(Pause.)* Uh-oh. Altitude. *(Tilts head back.)* Nosebleed! Oh, not now, now now — oh. Oh. OK. There. Maybe not. OK, I'm just light-headed, afraid of heights, or, when I'm up so high, I wonder what it would be like to jump. To fall. From so high a place. I'm attracted to the edge, you know. Closer, closer — a little closer. There is nothing to grab on to — nothing, just the sheer edge and then — aaaaaah-hhhhh! *(Pause.)* Does one — faint — before impact? Imagine being conscious, smashing into the earth — the body — the body — meeting absolute resistance? *(Pause.)* Mmmmmmm, smell the air up here! So clean and fresh — beyond their pollution, their noise, their — needs. Uh-oh, dizzy. Breathe! Breathe. Relax. Mmmmmmm. *(Pause.)* I've been coming up here for all the years of my life. Today that makes forty. Today I am forty years old. Of course, when I was very young, my father used to bring me up here. Only the altitude would make him irritable. He'd point out targets below and see if he could hit them with rocks. "See that weed over there," he'd say, "I'm gonna hit it with this rock!" All I could see was a large wildflower, orange like a rising sun. I thought it was beautiful. "Watch!" he'd say. Zing! I have to admit, he was pretty good. At that distance he could knock off quite a few petals — a skinny stem left shivering in the clear clean air. Then he'd point out to me where he worked, tell me again how much he hated it, how much he hated all the stupid, sheepy people he had to work with, how he was trapped — then he'd pick up really big rocks

1

and heave them into the air. "Thunk." Like a body hitting the earth, "thunk." Those rocks made such a hollow, heavy sound. "Thunk." Even before he died, I learned my way up here so I could be alone. The older I get, the harder the climb. And today, it's forty years of climbing. Look! Look how clear it is today. This is how Noah must have felt after forty nights, forty days of rain — to at last come to rest on the earth again. Looking around and everything clean and fresh and all his, all his! To populate! To go forth and multiply! What a job! What a great job! To create and create and create, morning, noon and night! Imagine! Surveying all that lies blow and knowing it's yours, all yours. That God is *definitely* on your side — there being no other side for Him to take — Forty years and here I am. Dry land at last. The ark has come to rest. My body touches the earth. And now what? Do I throw rocks or go forth and multiply? The fast way down is over the edge. *(Balances on one foot.)* "Look, Ma! No hands!" *(Pause.)* In the brief time it takes to fall, I imagine I am flying!

ALTER EGOS
Jon McGovern

Comic

> *Lerlene is a country-western glamour girl, twenties to thirties. This monologue is to the audience and is the first part of a much longer speech (in case you're looking for something longer . . .).*

> *Lights flash up as she turns and runs breathlessly downstage.*

LERLENE: Ohmigod! I just had this — *epiphany* — I think that's the word — it was like a flash of just knowin' — I had to get out! So, I just ran out of my trailer fast as I could — I only took my merry-go-round handbag and my two little dogs. I had to get out! The Bubbas were drivin' me crazy! When I say the Bubbas I mean my boyfriend Bubba and his two kids. *(Pause as the emotion builds up inside of her.)* Bubba *(On the pouty verge of tears.)* and Bubba — the man named his two sons the same thing — which woulda been fine if they hadn't been twins! Oh those kids! Always wantin' somethin' — especially not durin' my soap-opera slash talk-show hours! First of all . . . *(Her voice moves into her seductive range.)* I'm gonna be an actress. So soap operas are like crucial actin' lessons for me . . . *(A sudden switch back to the loud Lerlene we've met before.)* . . . and, second, I need to see the talk shows 'cause sometimes that's the only way I get to see my family! I mean, last week I missed my cousins BaSita and FaNita on *Jerry Springer!* Anyway, the main reason I left is . . . 'cause . . . well . . . *(Does a Wonder Woman–style twirl.)* I'm gon' be famous! . . . a supermodel/singer/actress — triple threat! And I need to be in a situation with a man who is going to support me in my career! 'Cause I'm on my way . . . I'm in training, I practice like, um, runway walkin' here in the trailer park . . . it's like . . . watch . . . *(Runs upstage and strikes her starting pose, then begins to walk.)*

One-two-work-bitch one-two and look and look and look and look . . . I do *Vogue* covers, it's like . . . chick chick *(She poses.)* Chick chick *(Another awful pose halfway between a cheerleading pose and a porno still.)* I'm ready . . . ready to be . . . discovered.

APRIL
Alison Fields

Dramatic

Eve is a single woman in her twenties, desperately seeking a commitment from a man. Here's she is talking about a man she recently met.

EVE: He helped me out. . . . I don't remember walking until I look up and realize I don't know where I am. And I guess it starts raining about that time. Summer shower, a regular downpour, and here I am in the middle of a neighborhood I've never been to in the dark, all alone. . . . So I find one of those covered bus stops and sit down to think about all that has happened. It occurs to me, only then, how crazy I'm acting, and I start to feel a little scared about where I am, and out of nowhere this guy walks up to me. . . .

    I don't know why. I just start talking, telling him everything about myself, about that night, and we sit together on that bench in the rain for hours, until the last bus stops for the night. He laughs and tells stories, and we smoke damp cigarettes from his pocket. I find myself falling for him almost automatically. When he invites me back to his apartment, I don't feel uncomfortable. It seems like the most natural thing in the world. He is safe and unsafe at the same time. And so different from David, and all the men at work. . . .

    . . . There was so much I didn't think about. Just start following him home in the rain. He lives in this old building in that neighborhood, up three flights of stairs. This big white room, mostly empty, except a couple of chairs and a sofa and a bed in one corner. He tells me he hasn't been in town for very long. We drink a bottle of cheap wine and talk until dawn and when the light shines through his windows we walk up to the rooftop and watch the sun reflect in the mirror buildings and I think I can see everything, past the city and to the bay. And we come back downstairs and make love. Sleep all day. Wake in the afternoon and make love again. . . . It was only after the second time that I finally asked his name. He said it was Simon.

AVOW
Bill C. Davis

Dramatic

Irene is an unmarried, pregnant woman in her thirties whose brother wants to marry his boyfriend in the Catholic Church. Here, she is making confession to their priest, to whom she is becoming increasingly attracted.

IRENE: Uh . . . The affair. You know — what I told you about. The married man. The reason I'm pregnant. I've been thinking about his wife. She is still in love with him. She suspected — she came to my apartment. I never answer the door when someone just stops by. I was in a good mood — I guess I thought it was Brian, so I just answered the door and . . . her eyes — they looked as if they were bleeding. I was so pulled together. I said, "Yes? What is it?" I knew what it was. It was hell. Hell was looking at me. Then out of nowhere she started laughing. And I thought, "Oh great — this is going to be a real episode." But she was laughing because she thought I was going to be a man. *(Pause.)*

She kept smelling someone else's aftershave on him. She told me that and then we both started laughing. She just couldn't figure out what mens' names begin with *I* because she saw my initials on a slip of paper. Then we started thinking up men's names that begin with *I.* "Irving," "Ignatius," "Isidore," "Ian." Then she suddenly got hysterical crying. I didn't know what to tell her. And I felt close to her because we had shared a laugh. I said I couldn't help her. I told her to talk to him about it. I had nothing to say. "This isn't about me. It's about you and him. It's not about me." *(Pause.)*

It was up to the two of them to keep their marriage alive and interesting and fulfilling. She wasn't giving him the kind of love he needed. *(Pause.)*

What do you want? You want me to feel responsible for her? *(Pause.)*

Godamnit! I do. I feel responsible for everything that will ever go wrong with her for the rest of her life. If she gets cancer, if she gets hit by a car, if she gets involved with a man that beats her — all of it will be my fault!

AVOW
Bill C. Davis

Seriocomic

> Avow *is about a gay couple who are trying to get the Catholic Church to bless their union with the sacrament of marriage. In this monologue Rose, sixty, is having lunch with her gay son and her unmarried, pregnant daughter. She doesn't know what to make of either of them.*

ROSE: *(Smiling.)* So — here I am with my gay son and my unmarried pregnant daughter. It's really exciting. I mean it's nothing that I expected, but the truth is that the unexpected things are the most important. Those are the things we learn and grow from. I mean, if I got a carbon copy of me and your father I'd have a son who'd want to have sex fifty times a day and a daughter who loves priests.
(Brian and Irene look at each other. Rose sees this.)
What? *(To Irene.)* You hate priests . . . *(To Brian.)* and you don't want to have sex fif . . ., well maybe you do, but I don't want to know. I don't need to know. I'm at peace about all of this because I listened to God the way Father Nash told me to listen. And God works much differently than I thought. He's very funny — and He doesn't try to make sense — He can't. That's not His job. There's no point to His trying to make sense to us — we have to make sense out of Him. *(To Brian.)* I started lighting candles that you'd get married and have kids, but then God straightened me out. He answered me by saying, "That's not the son I gave you." I almost heard him. "Relax — Brian is part of My equation. The world population has doubled in your lifetime, Rose, and this is how I'll slow things down." So I stopped lighting candles because I got an answer.

BANG
Laura Shaine Cunningham

Seriocomic

> *Sheila (thirties to forties) and her husband Len are visiting their old friend Bev and her new husband Roy, who live in an underground, nuke-resistant condo in (well, underneath) Utah. Here, she talks about Len's existential angst.*

SHEILA: . . . This is typical. On the way here, we stopped for lunch at a Howard Johnson's, and Len insisted that we park the car at a spot marked for the handicapped . . . you know . . . the signs with the little wheelchairs. I don't know why. There were plenty of spots. I said, "Len, it's going to be embarrassing when we get in and out of the car, and people see we're not crippled. It'll look like we were trying to hog a spot close to the restaurant." He wouldn't listen. Okay. So we had lunch, and when we came back out, he confessed: He's been using their toilets too . . . with the handlebars. He says they're bigger and better kept, but I think there's more to it. . . .

There's something really wrong with Len. Personally, I think it's totally linked to this economy. . . .

Well, just before we left, we stopped for cash at one of those outdoor bank slots. I don't know how we let it happen, but we were totally out of money, and it was midnight and there we were on Times Square . . . under a full moon. . . .

So poor Len put his card in and the machine spit back a message — "Transaction Not Completed." *(Her voice breaks.)* It swallowed the card too, then spit back another message, "Insufficient Funds." It was embarrassing — there were people behind us. It affected Len. He took it personally. It's too close to what he's been working on . . . his thesis "Psychonomics . . . Going Insane in a Crazy Economy." The truth is we've just been squeaking by. We're close to broke. Our

9

income is the same as our rent. I worked it out on a calculator and it costs us seventy-seven cents a minute to exist . . .

That's why I had to sublet the apartment. I hated to do it behind Len's back. But I found people to take it for more than we pay, so we can actually earn money by taking this vacation. We just couldn't go on. I mean, the meter is always running. I have to buy everything on charge cards. I use my American Express card to buy milk. I buy all our food at Zabar's. We're living on lox. It's eating away at Len, at his pride, or whatever you want to call it. Most days, he just sits on the sofa, shaking. He says, he's "quivering from the cost." Every morning when he wakes up, the first thing he says is: "Should I call in sick?" And I say "Don't be ridiculous, what would you do alone in this apartment all day?" And he says he wants to "concentrate." I know that he really watches infomercials on AB development. He starts to . . . babble . . . "just-lemme-alone-in-peace-and-quiet, just-lemme-alone-in-peace-and-quiet." To top it all off, he's almost totally impotent. He can only sustain an erection in his sleep. I've found a doctor who can diagnose impotence. A woman doctor. A friend of mine. She's an expert on impotence. And she's *offered* to strap electrodes to Len's penis and record his erections over a twenty-four hour period, but no. He refuses to accept any help. Let's face it, Len's in some kind of depression . . .

Len is in some kind of depression, and as long as it lasts, he's no use to me, to himself, or to you. So that's why we can't stay for dessert. He just won't be much fun until he finishes his thesis!

BEAUTIFUL BODIES
Laura Shaine Cunningham

Dramatic

A group of women, friends from college, now in their thirties, are at a baby shower for one of their number, Claire, who is (mysteriously) pregnant. Here, Claire tells the story of how it happened.

CLAIRE: He didn't comment we just greeted each other like old friends. . . .
    The candle burned low . . . we smoked a little grass . . .
    . . . and the room seemed all sparkly. The bubbles were iridescent; we played with them . . . Then we dried each other off . . . I have these big, rough towels that feel so good. I heat them on top of the radiator. . . .
    Then we went into the other room . . .*(She rises, moves away from the group, reenacting the memory. Soft to group.)* I can't look at you and tell you this . . .
    Well, I'll try. *(Softer.)* Oh I don't know what happened next . . . it gets fuzzy . . . I guess he turned on the radio. And I remember saying, "Would you like to dance?" And he said . . . in this really low voice . . . It was different from his usual one. . . . "Yes I'd like to . . ."
    (She looks down, caught in the spell of memory and the confidence. . . .)
    We never did dance. I think we took maybe one step. And that was it. We just stood there. It was as if we couldn't wait to start . . . kissing. I don't know . . . it seemed . . . momentous . . . but I think we could still laugh. My knees just went. I started to sink to the floor and then . . . he whispered it into my hair . . . so low, I couldn't understand a word except that he had asked a question . . . "Do you like . . . something or other?" And I said, "Yes" . . . *(Soft laugh.)* Apparently I was ready to agree to anything. Maybe he just said . . . "Do you like me?" *(She shakes her head.)* I don't know. . . . Anyway, I remember we were kissing . . . and I could feel the bristle on his upper

11

lip . . . the feel of his cheek against mine. . . . And then, well, it seemed accidental. Sometimes, it seemed as if we weren't moving at all . . . except for the tremble in our arms and then the tremble was inside, too, and . . . *(Her voice drops, she breaks off. Smile.)* We fell asleep on the floor and woke up later. It was very dark. I woke up first and watched him sleep. He must have somehow felt me watching — he opened his eyes right away. *(Softest.)* And I'll never forget how he smiled.

BINGO BABES
Isabel Duarte

Seriocomic

Mary is in her early forties. She is very bossy, very smart, and lives on welfare. Here, she is talking to a homeless person (whom we don't see) who may be her husband.

MARY: Good afternoon. *(Beat.)* I said, "Good afternoon!" *(She walks around, observing her surroundings.)* It's almost evening. Shouldn't you be up? How about sitting at least? . . .

Just want to make sure it's you. *(Beat.)* Don't get your feathers ruffled on my account. *(Beat.)* Fine. Be like that. Pretend I ain't here, But I know you can hear me. I saw you stir. . . .

Oh, don't be mad 'cause I haven't come in a while. You know how busy things get sometimes. I got two girls to raise, in case you've forgotten. . . .

Things are great with us, just like always. We're doing pretty good all things considered. There's only a small problem, and who doesn't have problems? I wouldn't even call it a problem; it's more like a rough patch. How's the sandwich? . . .

You're welcome. *(Beat.)* Look, I'm a little worried about our kids. What mother isn't? But I can't take it lightly, no way I'm gonna do that. This is one thing in my life that I got to get right 'cause I'm done havin' any more. What's there for me without my girls? Just Peg. Unless she keeps going out with Bag of Bones. That'll kill our friendship, that's for sure. Her and our girls are all I've got in this gigantic universe, which is more than most people got. But to hear Sharie talkin' earlier today, you'd think they hated how I am. What's not to like about me? *(Beat.)* Exactly, but just go ask our girls, and they'll come up with somethin'. When did Sharie start getting all those airs and Jen begin not spendin' any time at home? When? They got it into their heads to make me over, and I'm going to let 'em, otherwise . . . *(Beat.)* Look, I swore to myself that I wasn't going to do this ever again, but I'm going to try one more time. I don't miss you so much, but the kids do. I'm way over you, for years now. I ain't asking for me. Nope, not at all.

(Mary waits for a response.)

Come back. *(Beat.)* Think about it for a minute. . . .

Fine with me if you decide to turn down the offer your girls are making. I don't care. It's them you'd be hurting, not me. But if you do, it'll be the last time I come here pleading for them, that's for sure, so think about that. . . .

The good thing about you coming back home, should you decide to of course, would be that the girls would want to re-do you, and they'd help you too. I don't mean no offense, but you're the one who needs it more than me anyway. Just come home. We'll find some way of helpin' you. We'll walk back with our heads held high. Let's just walk back. *(Beat.)* I'm going to give you just a little more time to mull it over. *(Beat.)* Just another minute or two.

BLACK SHEEP
Lee Blessing

Comic

Elle, a woman thirties to forties, is describing a dream she has had to Carl, a visitor to her home. Her husband is a movie producer.

ELLE: I had the strangest dream last night. Do you dream? I only have night-mares. At least, I never remember happy dreams. Last night I dreamt that Max and I were in the guest house on the floor, and we were — *(Recoiling at the recollection.)* Oh, ugh. Oh . . . oh — ugh. Ugh! Why do we dream, Carl? I mean, why do we? *(After a beat.)* Max isn't so bad. It's just that he wants to make movies. And he's rich, so he can waste his time any way he wants. At first he got his father's friends to invest in movies he directed himself. Small budgets — a few million, nothing more — but still. They stunk so bad. Not horrendous. I mean, everybody's movies stink a little, right? That's just how movies are — they stink a little. But his. Really *stunk*. I should know, I'm in the business. I was the slutty one in *All the President's Hookers?* Did you see that? Not in prison I guess. Anyhow, by the time I met Max he was in another end of the industry. We hit it off right away. As friends, I mean. If he wants to nail me, we've gotta be married. I'm not like the other girls he's had — I get a ring. I mean, look at all this shit around here. Wouldn't you hold out? Max's family made some of their money in diamonds. Can you imagine the fucking ring? It's gonna happen, too. He really wants to do me. It's almost funny.

BLOWN SIDEWAYS THROUGH LIFE
Claudia Shear

Comic

> Blown Sideways Through Life *is an autobiographical one-woman show in which Ms. Shear describes in hilarious detail her multitude of subsistence jobs. This is one of them.*

CLAUDIA: I'm gonna study fencing with Mr. Barta. Advance advance advance retreat retreat retreat LUNGE. Putting aside the $23.00 I needed each week from the limp piles of my tip money. When I complained to Mr. Barta about his chronic lateness he said "Please Claudia, don't make a scenery." I run from work, my horrible proofreading cubicle, changing into my tights in the cold corporate toilet, running for the R to skid into the stinky woody floors of the Clark Center, the sound of the drums the drummers nodding nodding to the beat of the drums, the documents forgotten the fluorescent sweating itself out of my body as my teacher Charles Moore tells us "You have to dance like this, like you have a big jewel of your grandma's right here and you want everyone to see it" and if you hesitated and looked around he would say "don't look at your friends, your friends are wrong." Sneaking off the floor of the restaurant, "can you cover the last two deuces for me I've got to go to my French class." *Je dois aller a la l'ecole.* Running to my sanctuary at the Alliance Francaises, hunched over my exercise books with the ladies who lunch.

BLOWN SIDEWAYS THROUGH LIFE
Claudia Shear

Comic

> Blown Sideways Through Life *is an autobiographical one-woman show in which Ms. Shear describes in hilarious detail her multitude of subsistence jobs. This is one of them.*

CLAUDIA: I once had a job as a nude model for a painter — not just some guy, but a great painter — a grand, absolutely eccentric, obsessed painter — a genius, I think, with the occasional chilling gaze of the true monomaniac. "Art should have a smell — a smell — because then if it was bad . . . no one would have it in their house" I was always whining "C'mon give me a painting" "Give you a painting, give you a painting, I can't give you a painting — Do you know how important a good painting is? Do you know how much a good painting is worth?" "Well, give me a bad one" "No I can't do that." "Why not?" "Because — the bad ones are my enemies." Huge sky-lit studio with jazz on the radio and the whole place filled with this empty quiet light. It was the absolute safest place I've ever been, which is strange, I guess, considering I was buck naked on a large table piled with old bedspreads, the muscles in my back all tense and twisted and being really conscious of being really *naked* — feeling all breasts and skin and hair with someone — with a *man* staring at you that intently — Paul standing there, brushes in his hand and pockets absolutely still — stare stare stare soft grunt LUNGE PAINTPAINT-PAINT. It was *great.* You are actually part of the art as it's happening — like being a piano or a toe shoe. And to be beautiful — Oh I really loved being beautiful, not just pretty like a girl at a table at Raoul's wearing a size 6 dress from Barney's, laughing with her wineglass as her eyes flicker to see who is watching but beautiful, beautiful like a woman in a painting.

17

BOOK OF DAYS
Lanford Wilson

Seriocomic

> *Martha (about fifty), an ex-sixties radical, now teaches at the local college. She is very sardonic about the legacy of sixties "liberation" and what the new generation of young people has done with it.*

MARTHA: I can't for the life of me understand what the hell is going on with these kids today, I just saw a girl walking out of the pharmacy with her body pierced and stapled in every possible — rows of silver rings and studs through her lip, her cheek, her eyebrow, on her neck, her nose, her belly button — You know damn well she's got one on her clit . . .

    I'd like to see her drop *that* in a dish at airport security. And I'll bet you a dollar she'll be in my Freshman English Composition class this fall. Still they're not as bad as — I swear half my kids don't know they're alive. They live a calm, sexless denial of every human impulse. What is that? In the sixties we — well the late sixties, we rejoiced in our bodies, but the option now seems to be between self-mutilation and total denial of your existence. *(Mocking.)* And after all the indiscriminate sex and the endless ingestion of drugs we endured to set them free. We didn't put ourselves through those perilous experiments for ourselves. We did it for them. For our children. And our children's children . . .

    Good. Slopping barefoot and naked through the rain and mud at Woodstock. For what? Liberation! To make our country free! And look at what the Perforated Generation has done with it. I've got to get myself another story. I have thoroughly worn out Woodstock, haven't I?

BOYS AND GIRLS
Tom Donaghy

Seriocomic

> *This compelling comedy about same-sex parenting is about two couples: male/male and female/female. In this monologue Shelly, a woman in her twenties to thirties, is on the phone with her mother. During the conversation, she reveals that her girlfriend has left her.*

SHELLY: Hi, Mom, it's me. I wanted to go over the plans for your trip. I have the itinerary here. Because I paid for the tickets. I can send you a copy. It's just how they do it. It's just how it's done and there won't be confusion at the airport, no. I'll send you everything in advance. You'll have it *on your person.* So you're flying into Rome. No, it's just outside the city, it's — mmm — *(She looks.)* — it's called da Vinci, it's near the beach and then you — no, you're staying in the city in Trastevere. If Daddy wants to bring his bathing suit, fine, but Rome doesn't have a beach and the hotel doesn't have a pool. Should I be relaying all this to him, instead? Fine. You're welcome. You don't have to keep thanking me. Really, Mom, stop or we'll have to talk later. You sent me that jelly as a thank you and I don't have time for all this gratitude. And I think — you know what I think? Forget it. No — you know what I think? It's some fucked up way of making me feel guilty somehow for being able to treat you and Dad so well. Just accept it and be grateful, tell your friends and don't keep feeling the need to express this forced gratitude. *(She listens.)* She's fine. He's fine, he has the sniffles. Well, it's his birthday soon and then you can come over. No, he's on a business trip in Vancouver. He's been over extending a bit lately and he's been gone a lot and — no. We've hired someone. A nice guy who has training. He's Swiss so he keeps everything running. I know you like Reed, everyone likes Reed, but we need this professional who's more consistent. That is what is important for a child. *(She listens.)* Good, so everything's working out and you fly into Rome and from there a bus to Umbria. Which is beautiful. It's where Bev and I — when we first met and we couldn't afford Tuscany. I was still an associate and Bev was waitressing and we thought, ok, so not Tuscany, but someday! And then Umbria. So beautiful. How could Tuscany be better? And we thought maybe we found a, uh, new place. A new way. To do things. Based on disappointment. Which sets you off to someplace . . . unimagined . . . and — and — and — she's left me, Mom. She took Georgie. We were at the beach. I don't know what I've done. I yelled at Reed but I don't — I don't think that's it. It's been . . . I don't know what to do — we haven't been sleeping together and — what do I do? Mom? Mommy? *(She listens.)* Uhuh. Uhuh. Uhuh. Okay. No, okay. Okay, sure. Then — have a good trip. No, we don't need to talk before you go. I'll have Sonia send you all the info. She's my new assistant. She puts up with me, but I think it's cause I pay her. I just wanted everything you had with Daddy. That's all. Okay. Send him my love. And — and — to you too.

CONTROL FREAKS
Beth Henley

Comic

> *Sister Willard is a classic, eccentric "Henley-esque" character. She has what*
> *might be called (indeed is) Multiple Personality Disorder. She is about*
> *thirty. In this monologue, "SP" is Spaghetti, one of her other personal-*
> *ities. "P" is another, named Pinkie. Sister has no knowledge of Spaghetti*
> *or Pinkie. Pinkie is aware of Spaghetti, who knows all about Pinkie and*
> *Sister. Quite a challenge, eh?*

SISTER: *(Sister/Spaghetti/Pinkie.)* [SIS] Where's my face? Where's my face? What have they done with my face? I can't stand around here with- out a face that is not going to work, everything must work, let it work out. Please, I am begging you. Drench, drench. "Can't you straighten up and fly right?!" Fly — fly — / *(Sister races to the window. The noise from the shake machine stops.)* [SP] I fell out a window. I fell out a win- dow. I wanted to fall and crack open my skull./ [P] What would be inside? Oh, such surprises: tangerines, necklaces that sparkle, gold teeth, fine ribbon, chocolate wrapped in red foil. All my brains are treasures. How wonderful what I see. I could weep with joy. Rain- bow tears drift from the window. It's an outrage. Who will catch the tears? No one is below; I am crying colored tears and no one is below . . . I smell something. Something bad./ [SP] You don't./ [P] I can't help it, I do. I have to tell the truth. To thine own self be true./ [SP] I don't think so./ [P] I do./ [SP] Yeah? Well, you've never once gotten up and braved the light of day without lying your whole heart out. You tell yourself, I'm not gonna die; what I do is important; my life is good; I'm gonna have a nice day. Ah, ah, ah! That's better. Now I can rise to my feet soaked in the cum of canards and meet the day. Hello, day! Tweet, tweet. The birdies are chirping./ [P] Ooh, aren't those baby birdies sweet?!/ [SP] I'd like to snap their scrawny necks.

21

CONTROL FREAKS
Beth Henley

Comic

Sister Willard is a classic, eccentric "Henley-esque" character. She has what might be called (indeed is) Multiple Personality Disorder. She is about thirty. In this monologue, "SP" is Spaghetti, one of her other personalities. "P" is another, named Pinkie. Sister has no knowledge of Spaghetti or Pinkie. Pinkie is aware of Spaghetti, who knows all about Pinkie and Sister. Quite a challenge, eh?

Sister: *(Spaghetti/Pinkie.)* [SP] I gotta be careful. I gotta watch my mouth. Speaking in evil./ *(She slaps herself.)* [P] Don't hit me!/ [SP] Shut up! I will if I want to!/ *(She slaps herself and pulls at her hair.)* [P] Ow! Ow! Ow! Stop it! You're hurting me./ [SP] Then, shut up. *(She stops beating herself and sighs with exhaustion — as Sister.)* Oh goodness. Goodness. *(Tiptoeing around the yard.)* I don't know who I am anymore. There's this real sense I am lost. I have gotten lost. The path has disappeared and the berries have been eaten by the wren. I'm out here all alone and I can't even call because I don't know what name to call. Who would come and get me? What is I called for them and I called and then I was forsaken. *(The shrieking sound of cats howling blares across the sky.)* [SIS] My cats! Where are you? I hear you. Garfield? Plums? *(Sister discovers her two fat cats crammed in a tiny cage hidden between the bushes.)* Oh, there you are! Why, they've caged you up. Put you in a cage. Not to worry. Cages can be good. You have bars. Something to hold on to. Solid. You're not lost. You're there in the cage. People can watch you. But they can't touch. They may throw peanuts. Peanuts can hurt. But they can't kill. If you're in the cage. Good kitties. Good kitties. *(Sister returns the cats and goes to check her soggy underpants.)* Still wet. Dripping wet. I can't wear pants that are this wet. Dry, will you . . . I gotta doll up. I'm setting my cap for the guest. Carl'll be proud of me. He'll see I'm really good-looking. He'll see I can get a man.

CRUISING CLOSE TO CRAZY

Laura Shaine Cunningham

Dramatic

> *Carolee is a country singer (age flexible). Here, she is confiding to herself and to the spirits in the room.*

CAROLEE: *(Speaking nonstop, with broken energy.)* My mouth's so dry, I can't talk. *(Accelerating.)* Nine times in the hospital this year. Nodes. Ain't suppose to sing, that's how come I'm on the road, doing two shows a night, in thirty-six cities. I got letters from doctors all over the world, say, "Carolee, don't sing, don't speak, don't even open your mouth." There's one doctor so big, he's too big for the Mayo Clinic, that's how big he is, took one look down my throat, and said, "Don't even open your mouth for a year, Carolee, don't speak, even to me." *(Pause.)* So I kind of nodded at him, then went right back on the road, I can't do my people that way. God respects you when you work, but He loves you when you sing. *(She roots through the piled bedding.)* Where's my nerve pills? *(She finds a baggie, pops a pill.)* I thank God, I'm not on dope. *(She swallows a few more pills.)* This is just Percodan, for my back. *(She takes another one.)* Clears your head real good, too. I just had a sharp thought. *(She blinks.)* It was passing through. *(She shakes her head, woozy.)* Well, it'll come back. Always do. *(She gropes along the vanity shelf, accidentally knocks off one Styrofoam head.)* Didn't like that one much, anyway — I had another kind of nerve pill, it was better than most. It was the only one could stop my bad dreaming. *(She squints at audience.)* You ever dream you were dead? And it was so real, you was surprised to find you wasn't? Only you wake up, it ain't that different? *(She shivers.)* I have been having dreams so bad, I can't sleep. I'm afraid to put down my head, that's the truth. *(Shudder.)* I was wearing my violet dress, I was in a wine-color coffin, in a

23

wine-color room. Everybody in the business come pay their respects. They was all around me, whispering, "Oh ain't it sad, don't she look sweet?" But they was drinking beer and eating chicken legs, too. Earl Wayne. Norbie. The Duker . . . Honey Bascomb. They was all there, saying how great I was, but it was a bunch of bull. They were all just thinking — "Now, she's dead, even her old albums will sell." *(Thoughtful.)* Well, it worked for Elvis. He gone gold. *(Sigh.)*

I had to lie there, listening to all their bull, like they wasn't the ones put me right where I was. And they were saying, *(Imitation simper.)* "Oh, don't she look beautiful, ain't she finally at peace." Meanwhile, they got the new album piled up outside the funeral home door. Too bad I can't get out of my coffin and sign them. And you know, the entire time, the entire time, I'm just laying there, waiting for him to come in. *(She squints at the audience.)* And you know which one. There's only one ever really makes you crazy. Oh, there's some can get you going, make you a little nuts, but there's only one, can kill you. And don't you know? He don't even show. He done me dead like he done me alive. *(Angry.)* And now they want me standing next to him in the auditorium lined up with all a them, so we can be the Cavalcade of Fools . . . I can just see it. Him and me, crowned fools of country music, salutin' to our own stupidity. Winding up with *Amazin' Grace. (Croaking lyrics.)* "Oh, I'll fly away . . ." *(Bitter.)* I'll fly away, all right. I've flown. *(She shudders.)* I'm dying. This old bus is going to be my hearse. I'm dying, and there's nobody to care.

THE DEAD EYE BOY
Angus MacLachlan

Dramatic

> *Shirley is a "trailer trash" woman in her twenties with a possibly retarded son she had when she was fourteen and an abusive boyfriend. She is a drug addict and alcoholic. Here, she is doing the best she can to pray.*

> *Shirley sits alone, talking softly, casually.*

SHIRLEY: Thanks. Thanks. *(She giggles.)* That's all I can think of to — just — it's such a gift, God, I don't know what I've done — but — thank you. *(She takes a few breaths.)* Hmm. I've been thinking of Mr. Peebles. He needs help, man, really. He's been such a bastard to me. I know he hates women. I know he hates me. But I got to learn to keep my mouth shut around him so I don't lose this job, you know. So, if you could — I got to stop contradicting him in front of the customers. Even when he's completely fucking wrong and stupid and I know he'd make a better deal if he listened to me. — But I'm just the receptionist so — what do I know . . . But — if you could give him some wisdom. Or insight. You know? That would be good. And me a longer fuse. That would be really good. 'Cause — I don't want to blow it, you know — But he is such an asshole. *(She pauses.)* — Any of it. Umn. Can you — Can you — Um, just help me to believe in all this shit/stuff? More? Like . . . love. *(She giggles softly.)* You know. What Billy sees. You know? What my life could be. What it is, right now. All of it. 'Cause — you know I am, man. I'll be going along OK, kind of wobbly but pretty good, and then — bam — it's gonna creep up out of the basement and come up on me. This — thing — in me. And I — I really — I just want to get rid of it. I do. Kill it. 'Cause it's a motherfucker. God. *(She stops.)* So, what do I do? God? When it comes on. The voice. That crap. It's so ugly, and weak and — familiar. So — familiar — How can I change it? What do I do? I — I just feel like I'm — I know I'm "powerless over people, places and things" — I just — I need your help, OK? OK? Just — expand me. Expand my — heart. Tear it open. Go ahead. Just give me real strength — Not this bitch crap but — real. 'Cause I'm — I'm so — I'm just so afraid . . . it's going to — Just — What I want is — make me better. You know? Keep me going. Keep the door closed. Keep the dead *dead. (She pauses. Softly.)* For Billy. God. For my man. Who loves me. *(She breaks down.)* Don't let anything fuck it up. *(She stops herself crying.)* I'm just . . . scared I'm going to — That, you know, it's all just an illusion and he's really gonna get to know us and it won't be what he thinks we are and he won't like what he sees when he sees us, just like every other fucking man I ever brought — Fuck. *(She pauses.)* Make us clean. *(She stops.)* I'm so grateful, God. Thank you. I just want to believe in the good Shirley-Diane. The one he loves. That I don't even trust is there. 'Cause — God — I'm happy. *(She stops and laughs.)* Don't let any of us fuck it up. Anyone. Especially me. But. Anyone . . . OK? OK? OK. OK, man. Over and out. I love you. *(She smiles, crosses herself like a Protestant who's seen it in movies, bops up, and goes.)*

THE DEAD EYE BOY
Angus MacLachlan

Dramatic

Shirley is a twenty-three-year-old "trailer trash" woman with a nine-year-old son named Soren, to whom this horrifying monologue is addressed. She is very high and very drunk, and she slurs her words.

SHIRLEY: What do you do? Think. . . . Something spilled. Think. . . . No! Not your shirt. Something spilled. Think. . . . It's wet! . . . God. You use a paper towel. . . . Why do I even have to even tell you? . . . What are you — Don't use the sponge you clean the dishes with on the dirty floor. Think! Are you retarded? My God, Soren, are you a retard? *(She giggles.)* Do I need to take you to have your head examined? You're nine years old. . . .

You're not a baby. Oh — get up. Do I have to show you? Do I have to take you by the hand? Do I have to show you how? Like you were a baby? Come here. Come on. *(She takes him and drags him in the kitchen and stands in the doorway, pushing him in.)* Get it. . . . Just a couple. Rewind it. You got to think of trees. Soren. You know, they have feelings, man. And when they, when we kill all the trees, there won't be no air. And you'll kill everyone on this planet. You want that? What's wrong with you? Now wet one. *One.* One. . . . You're splashing all over! Wipe that up now. . . . You know I got this job interview. You start this on purpose. You're doing this on purpose, aren't you? You're torturing me on purpose. . . . Come on. Grab up those others now you pulled them off the — Think of the trees! Have some consideration for life, will you?! *(She jerks him by the arm back to the spill.)* Get down! *(She kneels down over him like two wrestlers ready for a match.)* What do you do now? . . . SOREN! Use what God gave you! You're not a vegetable! You've got a brain. Use it. You're not an idiot. What's wrong with you? What is the matter! Goddamnit. Wipe it. *(She bends over him and wipes with him. They almost look like two*

27

dogs humping — Shirley over him, on him.) Get. It. All. I've got to show you how to wipe up a spill? I'm supposed to be there by — Fuck, I'm telling you — no more Nestle's Quik. Ever. Never again. Never! Ever! Ever, ever! Over there — get it all, or it'll be sticky and draw ants. You want that? You want to live with ants crawling in your bed? You'll fall asleep and they'll get in your ears and eat your eardrums and crawl up in your head and eat your brain out. I had a friend that happened to — she was . . . *(She pulls him up.)* Are you smiling at something I said? Goddamnit, I'll wring your fucking neck. What did I say? . . . I was making sense, wasn't I? Come on. Fuck. What did I — Wasn't I? *(She jerks him around to face her, then she shrieks.)* Oh shit! Oh no. Goddamnit! You just got it on me! *(She throws the paper towels down and stands.)* There's a spot on my fucking skirt! I got a spot! There's a spot. I got a spot. Hand me that — I got nothing else sexy to wear! . . . Don't! Stop it. Why are you doing this? *(She bursts into tears.)* Why did I — I'm so stupid stupid! *(She grabs him and shakes him over and over.)* Why do you hate me? You're a monster!

THE DYING GAUL
Craig Lucas

Dramatic

Elaine, a woman in her thirties, directly addresses the audience about a problem in her marriage.

ELAINE: The screening turns out to be surprisingly interesting, a project Jeffrey fought for under the old head of production — and the scores are good, and we all ride back together and laugh and celebrate our new friendship and their joint project, and after we drop Robert off, after we get back and put the children to bed and Jeffrey and I have made love, he was unbelievably *excited.* Jesus, it's . . . it's a little . . . well, it's new having him enthusiastic about . . . another human being . . . not just sex, I mean, but . . . and it's another, possibly one more part of his life I won't get to share in. Oh, I know Jeff likes men. And I've never minded what doesn't threaten . . . us. But . . . the way he kissed me . . . just now . . . I have to find some way in, a means to join in whatever it is they . . . have or don't have . . . A way — . . . Well, I don't have to decide what it is I'm going to be exactly, do I? I find my little online manual . . . with the house dark and all of the valley stretched out and flickering like phosphorescent fish, the tiny lights on the sound system and the fax machine, the security system, the pool, the walkways, all the faint glowing electric underpinnings of our lives which hint at the excitement I feel as I figure out how to make up a new screen name . . . and sign on now as: *(Types into her laptop.) Skinflute7.* Profile: "33. Venice Beach. Landscape architect." Find my way to *Men4MenParkBench.* I know he has to have a more salacious moniker than *Rob131,* but is it one of these? *MrThick:* Medical professional. *HornyZook:* Favorite quote: "If I blow your mind, you have to promise not to think in my mouth." I don't think so.

FROZEN STARS
David Matthew Barnes

Dramatic

> *Amy, twenty-two, is a college student who is desperately in love with a self-destructive man. Here, she is telling the concerned mother of her boyfriend why she is so worried about her son's dangerous behavior.*

AMY: What am I supposed to do? I know he's in trouble. And he won't stop. I told him once that he was the man I wanted to spend the rest of my life with — and it's true. He's different than anyone I have ever known. The guys I went out with before were all about money and their cars and how much their daddy did for them. I didn't want danger, but I wanted something more. My friends think I'm crazy for going out with Carlos. They don't understand it. To them, they just see a Mexican, a drug dealer, a thug. But Carlos is good to me. He's just really messed up right now. And I'm scared. I'm scared of the fighting and the drugs and the guns and the sound of Carlos crying when he thinks I'm asleep. I keep thinking about what I would do if he got killed. That's why I'm coming to you, Gloria. You're his mother. I need your help. If we don't save him — Why is it so difficult for him to see beyond all of this? Okay, so he doesn't want to be some corporate guy in a tie. I'm fine with that. But he's so much better than all of this. He's so smart. He just doesn't believe in himself. He doesn't believe me when I look at him and I tell him that I love him. He just thinks I'm some crazy white girl who felt sorry for him. But I'm telling you, Gloria, I love Carlos more than anything or anyone in this world and I don't want him to die. I need you to help me. For me. For him . . . and for my baby. I don't want to be a widow, Gloria. I just want to be in love.

FROZEN STARS
David Matthew Barnes

Dramatic

> *Lisa is an eighteen-year-old woman: intelligent, articulate, ambitious, and emotionally strong. Here, she is in a Mexican restaurant telling her boyfriend Eddie why she is so determined to go away to college, despite his objections.*

LISA: You're wrong! I'm fucking scared! I don't wanna end up like my mother. I see her face every day of my life and it makes me sick inside. I just look at her and I see my future. If I stay here, she is what I will become. She hates her life, because she never had one. There's nothing left of my mother but a broken heart. *Esta muerto!* She married my father because she didn't have a choice. But I do! I'm getting the fuck outta here, while I still can — and if you can't understand that, then it's your own damn fault! No man is going to hold me back from what I want — not now, not ever! Chances like this — they don't come along every day for a girl like me. Look at where I come from! Look at my family! My brother is either locked up or fighting in the streets! My mother has to clean houses for the rest of her life! My father can't even read and he hates the world! I'm not going out like that! I don't want to be a fucking statistic! . . . I never wanted to hurt you. Believe me. I love you, Eddie Cervantes. I wouldn't have the courage to do this without the faith you put in me. But I need you to understand this.

FROZEN STARS
David Matthew Barnes

Dramatic

> *Miss Carlisle (twenty-eight) is a high school guidance counselor who truly cares about her students. Here, at a women's medical clinic, she tells one of her female students about her past.*

MISS CARLISLE: It's going to be okay, Lisa. I'll be right here when you get back. You won't be alone — not like I was. The smell of this place reminds me of when I was here. I was three years younger than you, but just as ambitious. I was fifteen and I got pregnant — by my brother's best friend. His name was Freddie and he had the cutest dimples I had ever seen. His front tooth was chipped and he was a little shorter than me, but that didn't matter. What mattered is that I had a boyfriend. That finally, somebody had picked me and I felt special. He made me feel beautiful and I had never felt that way before. He worked at an ice cream parlor by our house. He used to bring me blueberry milkshakes. Everyday after work, he'd come over to our house. I used to watch from my bedroom window upstairs. I would sit there and wait until I saw him walking up my driveway. And he always had a blueberry milkshake, wrapped up in a brown paper bag for me. Things got crazy because the first time we had sex, I got pregnant — what luck. Freddie wanted to marry me, because he felt it was the right thing to do, but I didn't love him. I didn't love anybody — I was only fifteen. My mother was there for me through the whole pregnancy. She convinced me that giving the baby up for adoption was the best decision. I can't say that I regret it. I mean, I was so young and there was so much that I wanted to do. I didn't want to spend the rest of my life in the ghetto. So I gave the baby away. I never even saw her. But I heard her cry. In fact, sometimes . . . I still hear it . . . the sound of my baby crying.

GIVE ME YOUR ANSWER, DO!

Brian Friel

Dramatic

Daisy, a woman in her early forties with a severely retarded daughter, is here talking about an offer her cash-strapped novelist husband has had for his manuscripts from an American university.

DAISY: Oh, no, he mustn't sell. Of course he mustn't sell. There are reasons why he wants to sell and those reasons are valid reasons and understandable and very persuasive. A better place for Bridget. Escape from the tyranny of those daily bills and the quick liberation that would offer. Maybe a house with just a little comfort. And if David's offer is as large as he suggests, then of course the most persuasive reason of all: the work has value — yes, yes, yes! Here is the substantial confirmation, the tangible evidence! The work *must* be good! I'm not imprisoned in the dark anymore! Now I can run again! Now I can *dare* again! *(Pause.)*

Yes, it is so very persuasive. I convinced myself I believed in all those arguments, too — I think because I knew they were so attractive, almost irresistible, to him. But we were both deluded. Indeed we were. A better place for Bridget? But Bridget is beyond knowing, isn't she? And somehow, somehow bills will always be met. And what does a little physical discomfort matter? Really not a lot. But to sell for an affirmation, for an answer, to be free of that grinding uncertainty, that would be so wrong for him and so wrong for his work. Because that uncertainty is necessary. He must live with that uncertainty, that necessary uncertainty. Because there can be no verdicts, no answers. Indeed there *must* be no verdicts. Because being alive is the postponement of verdicts, isn't it? Because verdicts are provided only when it's all over, all concluded.

Of course he mustn't sell.

And now I'm going to pour myself a little gin. And only half an hour ago I made a secret vow to give up gin forever and ever and to switch to health-giving red wine But there you are — the road to hell — touch of a slut — and so we stagger on — . . . To the Necessary Uncertainty.

HOMECOMING
Lauren Weedman

Dramatic

> Homecoming *is a one-woman play in which the actress plays several different roles. Here Lauren, a teenaged girl, is talking to her adoptive mother, Sharon, about who her birth mother might have been.*

LAUREN: I wanted to ask you about my *real mom.* . . . There! That was easy! . . .

No, you know what I'm talking about. And, I'm not asking because it's some like, big huge, like trauma for me or something. It's not that. Because if anything, mom . . . I'm proud of it. You know, like in school, when we come back from summer vacation . . . and the teacher asks everybody, "So, what'd you do over your vacation?" I'm always like, "I'm adopted." And everybody goes "oh my god, adopted girl." "Can I borrow your pencil adopted girl?" So, it's not that it's some big . . . it's just that um, it's just that I um . . . I don't know what I look like. Ya know what I mean? It's like every time I see a picture of myself I look like this big white squish. And, well, people at school keep asking me about it. Like, like, like Wendy and Grandma. Grandma said you tried to get my medical records for me because you were scared I was inbred or something like that. So, ya know, have you found those? Or maybe a picture of my birth mother somewhere. Um, that you hadn't given me. And mom . . . mom . . . if you did have a picture somewhere — I wouldn't obsess it or anything. If that's what you're scared about. I won't always be walking around, all the time, thinking like, oh my God, there she is. Or building a shrine around her or something . . . I'd just like to have it to have in a drawer someplace, just to look at once in a while. It'd be no big deal. I just think that whatever information you have, I'd, I'd, I'd like to know it. Okay? So whatever you know, I think I'm ready.

HOMECOMING
Lauren Weedman

Comic

> Homecoming *is a one-woman play in which the actress plays several different roles. Here Lisa, a teenager, is talking to her sister, Lauren who, apparently, has serious identity issues and packs a few pounds.*

LISA: Lauren, how did you get into Black Student Union? Don't you have to be black? Well, do they know you go to Hebrew School? And they don't care?

Listen, I just wanted to tell you that if you decide that you're going to search for your real, um your, um birth-biological-whatever I don't know what you call them. Okay! I just hope you're not doing this because of what Grandma says. Because she's crazy, Lauren! Yes she is. She tied mom to a tree.

I don't know if I ever told you this or not, but for a long time I thought you were like a foster child that was just staying with us for a while until your family came and got you? And when I found out that you were really my sister, and you were staying, I was so happy. Okay? And that's always how I felt about you. So whatever you decide . . .

Is that my sweater? Is it?!! You're not to wear my things. No, you are not! Will you take that off please, fold it and put it outside my door. And fold it nicely. Arms crossing, like this.

(Begins to weep.) I love you. Okay? And that's what I wanted to tell you. So, you need to hurry up and change your clothes, because mom's waiting downstairs to take you to Weight Watchers.

JAR THE FLOOR
Cheryl L. West

Dramatic

Raisa, thirty, is the only white character in this drama about four generations of black women. Here, she is talking to Madear, the great grandmother of her friend Vennie, to whom she reveals that she has cancer.

RAISA: I hear it Mrs. Dawkins but you know how I keep it at bay? Everyday I go to Europe, in my mind. I'm buying me some mean Italian shoes and I'm sitting in one of those little cafes all day philosophizing, smoking cigarettes, drinking exotic coffees and wines. You wanna hear today's trip? . . . Okay, I'm sitting outside a little café and I'm wearing a black beret, kind of cocked to the side with a big diamond butterfly pen right in the middle. I used to dream in zirconia, but these days this girl's dreaming in diamonds. Anyway, I got this huge diamond right smack in the middle of my beret. I'm a beacon of rainbow color. You picturing me now, aren't you? . . . Okay, so I got this brilliant light radiating off my forehead. It's just about blinding to anybody who comes within a hundred feet. So of course everybody has to stop and ask, where'd you get such a magnificent pin? And I laugh oh so haughtily . . . *(Demonstrates her auteur laugh and accent.)* "Oh this ol' thing . . . well darlings, it's just my latest creation." And they're speechless, utterly, utterly entranced with me as they move closer, . . . their eyes scanning my body, up and down, left to right, head to toe and they're transformed. Yes, you can see it on their faces. Did I happen to mention except for the body paint, I'm stark naked while all this is going on? *(Raisa laughs . . .)* Oh yes, and then the clapping starts. It's feverish with excitement. *(Clapping her hands to demonstrate.)* Magnifico! Magnifico! I think that's how you say it but anyway, they're throwing flowers at my feet. It's unanimous. They have declared me a work of art. Raisa Krementz's body is a work of art! *(Touches the place of her missing breast.)* Even here. *(Beat.)* God, I wanna

37

go. I really, really wanna go. I can almost taste it. Even it's only for a day. *(Beat.)* They found a new spot on my liver. The doctors said it's chemo time, but I said no, it's Raisa's time and Raisa's not in the mood to share a second of it with chemo . . . not now. I just want to get away, to have a piece of my dream before it's too late.

JAR THE FLOOR
Cheryl L. West

Dramatic

*This is a play about four generations of black women. In this monologue
Maydee, a woman in her mid-forties, is chastising her daughter,
Vennie.*

MAYDEE: Bullshit Vennie! Six years and three schools later, you still haven't
finished. You don't like the teachers . . . you don't like the school . . .
you don't like their politics . . . so you just up and quit. One semes-
ter left and you quit. Again! Just like you do every job, every apartment . . . What do you have to show for my thirty-five thousand two
hundred and thirty something dollars? . . . Nothing! No paper. No
graduation. No skills. Nothing! Your damn dream! Well, if you're
going to Europe, baby, you're going on a wing and a prayer because
your behind's not getting another dime from me. You got some kind
of gall even asking . . . This was supposed to be my day and you
wouldn't even let me have that. My entire family was supposed to be
here to support me. Me! You do understand the meaning of that word,
don't you? The one moment in my entire sorry life that I've been
happy and you robbed me of even that. Just snatched it away with
another one of your simple-ass whims to get my money. Well I'm not
letting you rob me of another damn thing, Vennie. You hear that?
Did you give one thought to me or your great-grandmother who's
turning ninety today . . . bringing her a bag of damn dirt. Did you
really think some cheap ass T-shirts and some half-dead weeds were
enough to seal the deal . . . ? And what was Raisa for, your poster
child?

THE LAST CARBURETOR
Leon Chase

Dramatic

> *Karen, in her late twenties, is a former physics student who recently dropped out of graduate school. Now she works full-time as a waitress in a truck stop near her hometown in southeast Michigan. Keith, her former lover who left nearly a decade earlier for California, has unexpectedly shown up at the truck stop. At this point, the two have sat down and begun to get reacquainted, and Karen is attempting to explain why she quit school.*

KAREN: *(Snickering.)* You wanna talk about the big picture? One night, a couple winters ago. It was snowing. I was out getting coffee with a bunch of people from my department. Serious quantum mechanics geeks. And let's be honest, Keith, none of these people grew up on *our* side of town. You know what I mean. Expensive lattes and shit. So we're there, and we're all sitting by the window, going off about what we thought about this presentation on theoretical black matter. Everybody's going out of their way to be real important, you know, all talking over each other. And I look outside, and right in front of us, on the other side of the big window, is this woman. Could be thirty, could be sixty. Obviously homeless. She's got on this pink coat, all dirty, and some kind of scarf on her head. Bags by her feet. She's just standing there in the snow. And she's screaming. I don't mean just like begging. I mean she's screaming, out loud. I realize that the people with me, inside, notice her too, but they're trying hard not to look. They're going along with this conversation, you know, staying really involved in this argument. Because nobody knows how to deal with a nontheoretical, live screaming human. I tried to look away. I mean, I really tried to focus and make myself forget about it. But all I could think was how stupid we sounded. After that, I just couldn't buy it anymore. I can't explain it. I just couldn't . . . I couldn't believe in it.

LIMONADE TOUS LES JOURS
Charles L. Mee

Dramatic

> *Jacquelyn, a charming and lovely French woman in her twenties to thirties, is talking to Andrew, a middle-aged American man with whom she is having a romance. We are in Paris.*

JACQUELYN: Oh, no, he's much too old for me. . . .
I think he's forty. . . .
You can understand. . . .
I mean, not that I have anything against older men
quite the opposite in a way
only I was married to an older man
and he took such a patriarchal position
and then I
I found I liked it
I invited it
so we had almost a sado-masochistic relationship
which I found I just loved
he had other lovers
he treated me like dirt
he wanted always to handcuff me to the bed
and it seems I not only fell into a sort of dependent role
but I had sought it all along
so now
I'm trying to go straight
you know
grow up
have a relationship with another grown-up person
as a grown-up person
if I have any relationship at all
and at the moment I don't have one at all

and don't want one
because I'm still recovering
and you? . . .
I don't know.
Maybe this is not the place to forget about love. . . .
Or else maybe it's a nice place to remember how it is to be alone
and to be starting out in a new world
where anything could be possible again
where you don't know what might happen next . . .
Because when you come to the end
you need to get back on the horse . . .
I have moved into a new place
which I love.
Of course, I am very lonely
because after you live with someone
you are used to not being alone
even if you hate him and he is disgusting
and picks nothing up from the floor
so that even when you get out of bed in the morning
you slide on a pile of magazines and fall to the floor
and hit your head on the edge of the bed.
But my new place,
it is all mine.
Very simple.
I have a fireplace
a shaded lamp
a box of stationery
a lounge with a mess of cushions of all sizes
a very simple bed in a separate room
and of course my coffee table
made from an old pheasant trap.
Do you now what a pheasant trap is? . . .
No, neither do I.
It looks like a large
what would you say?
A footlocker

two footlockers together
but made of wood
with little bars, like a wooden bird cage
where you can keep your pheasants
I don't know why
maybe to keep them there
until you set them loose so you can shoot them
I don't know.

And then that delicious feeling of being alone
when you are alone in your new home
and lonely
that feeling that feels sometimes like soaring freedom
at other times like retribution almost,
do you know?
You are being punished for what you did wrong
or didn't do quite right
and sometimes it is a heavy crushing feeling
that makes you want to hit your head against the wall.
So you are looking for a young woman
half your age?

LIMONADE TOUS LES JOURS
Charles L. Mee

Dramatic

> *Jacquelyn, a charming and lovely French woman in her twenties to thirties, is talking to Andrew, a middle-aged American man with whom she is having a romance. We are in Paris.*

JACQUELYN: The thing is
   when I was a girl
   my father was dying of alcoholism
   and my mother took me away from him
   and married another man
   and I grew up without my father
   missing him
   so that when he died
   I ran way from home
   and I lived in a car parked next to his grave
   and mourned for him and missed him

   but when you think this might be an explanation for things
   that happened later in my life
   you can always think of one or two or three big reasons for anything
   you do
   and then probably you have a hundred little reasons
   you can't even remember them all
   but they come back to you
   in different clusters
   so that finally you have so many explanations for things
   you can't know anymore what is true
   and your own inner self
   like the inner selves of everyone else
   just remains a mystery.

Sometimes a woman will want the love of an older man
she is captivated by an older man
she wants to be a daddy's girl
this is so common
you might almost consider it normal
even though it's wrong.

One time when I was nineteen years old
riding home in a cab with an older man
I found myself begging him to kiss me.

L-PLAY
Beth Henley

Seriocomic

Shelly, a woman in her twenties, is in a bar talking to Wes (about her age). The Ben she mentions is an older man who's her boyfriend. Little does she know that Ben has "bestowed" her on Wes.

SHELLY: Don't tell anybody, but Ben made this pie, a lemon ice-box pie, and I think he squeezed in too many lemons or didn't remember how many eggs, because overnight it didn't gel. It just stayed real liquidy. And I said don't worry, we'll just say it's custard; but he said it's supposed to be a pie. So we went on and took it to the Rodeo Picnic and set it out on the dessert table, and nobody ate it. I should of gone by and taken some pieces just to be nice, but there were all these other really good desserts: cherry cobbler, fudge brownies, homemade ice cream. At the Women's Crisis Center, they try to teach you it's healthier not to pretend to eat pie and secretly sling it in a trash barrel just to make somebody like you. But I think I'd be happier if Ben wasn't mad at me and I didn't feel like I was awfully mean and selfish not to even go by and take one piece of his pie. He worked hard making it. He wanted it to turn out good. It broke my heart because he pretended like it didn't matter when he came back and found out his was the only dessert on the whole table no one had even touched. I'm sorry I was talking fast. I been eating candy; I better shut up.

LOOKING FOR NORMAL
Jane Anderson

Comic

Patty Ann is a teenager, speaking in her sex-ed class.

Lights up on Patty Ann standing in front of a medical chart showing a cutaway of the female reproductive organs.

PATTY ANN: This is what happens when the female body matures. At around age twelve — younger if you've been drinking milk from chemically treated cows — your glands start pumping estrogen into your body which is what makes your breasts develop and hair grow in disturbing places. And your ovaries — which are here — get bigger and bigger and the follicles inside them start to swell until one of the pops like a water balloon and drops an egg into the fallopian tube. In the meantime, your uterus — here — is swelling up like a big bloody sponge, getting ready for the egg to drop. And if there's sperm in there when it happens, the egg gets fertilized and it sticks to the lining of the uterus like a burr on a sock and there's no frigging way you'll ever be able to shake it off. But if you're still a virgin, then the egg keeps going and the uterus says, "Okay, nothing going on, don't need this," and it lets go of the lining and all this blood starts pouring out of your crotch along with mucous and big hunks of dead tissue. And you have to wear a sanitary napkin so you don't have all this stuff running down your leg and if you don't change the napkin often enough it starts to stink like bad meat and everyone will know you're having your period. Along with that you can get cramps, headaches, diarrhea, hideous bloating and hundreds of pus-filled zits breaking out across your face. You can also get depressed, paranoid, and so completely strung out that you start weeping uncontrollably in public places. Some girls love getting their periods, it's like, "Oh, I'm a woman now, aren't I special." This doesn't interest me. I wish I were a guy.

When guys mature, they get muscles. They get meaner and leaner while we get these big blobby boobs and butts that bounce around and weigh us down. I've been told that it's possible to delay sexual development. For instance, girls who are competitive gymnasts or ballet dancers don't get their periods until they're nineteen or twenty. Our P.E. teacher says that what happens to these girls' bodies is abnormal. Me, I think it's a frigging miracle.

MONTHS ON END
Craig Pospisil

Comic

> *Heidi, twenty-two, is giving a college commencement address. For your purposes, though, she could be eighteen and delivering a high school commencement address.*

MAY

> *"Pomp and Circumstance" plays as the lights come up, and Heidi, a nervous young woman wearing a black graduation robe, enters and crosses to a podium. She carries a small stack of three-by-five note cards, which she refers to as she speaks.*

HEIDI: Welcome. Welcome friends and family, welcome to our teachers . . . and welcome to our parents. *(Slight pause.)* The day has finally come. The day this graduating class has been working toward for so many years of hard study. And I think I speak for my entire generation when I say . . . thank you. *(Slight pause.)* Thank you to our parents. The people who lit the way. Who loved us and nurtured us. And who now cheer us on as we set out to face the challenges of tomorrow. *(Pause.)*

This class stands before you today poised to — *(The cards in her hand suddenly fly into the air, scattering around the podium. Heidi freezes and then looks at the cards lying around her on the floor. She tries to continue from memory.)* . . . ah, poised to take on those challenges. We greet them with open arms. *(Pause.)* We, ah . . . stand . . . no, um . . . *(She glances down to the cards on the ground, turning her head around to try and read some of them.)* It's wonderful for me to be able to stand here like this . . . and look out . . . Hold on, I'm sorry. *(Heidi stoops down and collects the cards, pulling them together randomly. She stands and smiles nervously at the audience.)*

And in those faces I see hope, idealism and . . . no, that's wrong. *(She flips to the next card.)* We have spent four years at this school, studying hard and playing hard. And all of it has been part of our education, because — *(She goes to the next card.)* If you scratch our collective surface . . . damn it. I'm sorry. I guess I should have numbered them. *(Next card.)* Welcome . . . no, did that one. *(Next card.)* Because college isn't just about reading Shakespeare or understanding the Theory of Relativity. These four years have been part of our evolution from adolescence to — *(Next card.)* . . . a feeling of great loneliness . . . *(Pause.)*

I'm very sorry. Just give me another moment. *(Heidi quickly spreads the cards out on the podium and reorders them. She begins again.)* All right . . . The day has finally come. The day this class has been working toward for so many years of hard study. And I think I speak for my entire generation when I say . . . oh, what's the point? *(Pause.)*

I mean, it's ruined, right? *(Slight pause.)* This is all my parents' fault. I was fine until they came by my room this morning, and my dad says to me, "Make it good, Heidi, Make sure they remember you." *(Slight pause.)* How's this? *(Slight pause.)*

Not that the speech was much good to begin with. I know these things are supposed to have a theme, but . . . I mean, it's all been said already, hasn't it? And I'm sorry, but today just doesn't feel that momentous or anything. I know it's the end of one thing, and the start of something else, but so what? Everything's like that. *(Slight pause.)* I don't know why I'm up here. I didn't want to give this address. Hell, I didn't even want to come to this college! I liked Vassar! But my dad went here. "It's a great school, Heidi. When you graduate from a place like this you can get a job anywhere." *(Pause.)*

Which would be great, if I had the slightest idea what I wanted to do with my life. *(Slight pause.)* I think that's the symptom of my generation's disease. We're caught between optimism and nihilism. You raised us to believe in limitless possibility. Consequently we have no idea how to choose anything. *(Slight pause.)* Not that there seems to be much point. The country is, what . . . trillions of dollars in debt? And who knows if there will be any social security left by the time I retire, so why think about the future? *(Pause.)*

There'll be peace, you said. And racial harmony, sexual equality.

Diseases will vanish. *(Pause.)* Uh-huh. *(Slight pause.)* Yeah, this from the people who were gonna save the world, but then decided to make a bundle on Wall Street instead. Kind of an oxymoron, don't you think, Mom? *(Slight pause.)* Was it too hard? Or did you just get bored? *(Pause.)*

And you wonder why we get tattoos and pierce our belly buttons, or eyebrows, or whatever. We're pissed off because you lied to us. *(Slight pause.)* Well, mainly, we're angry, because you took all the good drugs, had all the good sex, and then made all the good money. *(Slight pause.)* The only thing you're leaving for us is the bill. *(Pause.)*

I should probably stop here. *(Heidi looks over the cards on the podium and chooses one.)* And so, in closing, this class would like to say a heartfelt . . . thank you . . . to our parents. Thank you for loving us and taking care of us. *(Pause.)* We look forward to returning the favor in thirty or forty years. *(She exits. Fade to black.)*

NOVEMBER
Don Nigro

Comic

This comic drama, one of the (chronologically) last in Nigro's extraordinary Pendragon Cycle, takes place in a retirement home. Mrs. Prikosovits (elderly) is one of its rather more whacked-out residents. Here, she is talking to another resident.

MRS. PRIKOSOVITS: I saw that woman that what's her name that Rooks woman used to be Johnny Palestrina's wife Becky, we used to live across the alley from those Palestrina people, his people, and before that she was married to that man who hung himself in the barn and now this Rooks person who is if you ask me a kind of jungle person but those Palestrinas were nice Italian people. Raphael and Anna and Anthony the big one he was the boxer and Rosa his pretty little sister could catch Johnny's spitball and Gina the wild one she wasn't really bad she just had large breasts of course mine was larger but I was fat all over before my many sicknesses and my boy Eddy took her out behind the brickyard when her brother Anthony found them in the blackberry bushes oh that was sad and them boys would play baseball out by the mill and Johnny was the best but after the war he married that woman who was here the other day I just said her name and then I forgot but we're all stupid when you come right down to it look at me I married Elmo but who was she? . . .

Your knees, yes. I have trouble with my knees, too. Lordy, mine buckle like a belt, I stumble around like a hoppopitamus and I remember Elmo would punch me in the face when I ate the last doughnut in nineteen thirty-five he hit me with the garden hose he was such a pig I loved him so, I remember on our wedding night he was so gentle it was because he didn't know what the hell he was doing but of course I did although we each had to pretend otherwise we were after all only babies. . . .

I've forgotten all about him he's awfully dead now and you know I was saying to that skinny nurse what is her name, Jane, Nurse Jane like Uncle Wiggly's mistress who was a muskrat I think and he was a rabbit we used to read to the children and she'd be pretty if she didn't always look like she was running a marathon race I said to her as she was giving me my enema I said, Nurse Wiggly, I said, if God loves me why does he make me pee at the wrong time?

NOVEMBER
Don Nigro

Seriocomic

Aunt Dor is an elderly woman who has been unable to speak since she was very young. Here, she says what she'd like to say, if she could speak.

AUNT DOR: Poor old Lizzy. Time and again Lewis used to say to Molly or Molly would say to Lewis, if Dorothy could only talk, she'd certainly have some tales to tell, all the things she's seen. They were right, of course. When you can't hear and you can't talk, people tend to treat you like a child or an idiot. It's remarkable how they come to forget you're there. I guess, it's like using the toilet in front of the cat — at first it bothers you, with those little eyes staring at you, but after a while you get used to it and forget all about them. I've been much forgotten about, in my time. I've lived a mostly forgotten life. But I've learned to hold out for those things which are really important to me, and to be very stubborn about those few things, and let the rest of it just go hang. I insist on watching Monday Night Football, and no matter how bad Molly wants to see some stupid Tyrone Power movie, I stick to my guns, and in the end she gives in. Also, I need my Canton Repository in the afternoon, I absolutely require it, and I had my old rocker from the farm brought to Molly's so I could rock and read the paper in the afternoon as I always have, with the cat on my lap. The cat is mandatory, although this stupid cat of Molly's is not much of a cat when you've had the privilege of rocking for ten years of long afternoons with John Foster Dulles on your lap. John Foster Dulles, I feel, was probably the most extraordinary cat in the history of tomcats, and it was my privilege and honor to serve under him, literally under him, from the day he wandered onto the porch as a gawky young tom — poor Lizzy, you never could turn anybody away hungry, stray cats and half-dead raccoons — until the day Ben went off to college and John Foster jumped down off the porch swing, marched over and shat in the front seat of Rooks' new pickup truck, on the driver's side, and then marched off across the road and up the hill into the woods and disappeared forever. I expect he knew when it was time to get out. Cats do. I never saw him again, but I approved heartily of what he'd done. If I could have climbed up into the truck, I'd have done it myself. John Foster had moral courage and a sense of righteous indignation of the very first order, and I salute him, today, wherever he may be, in cat heaven or elsewhere. But I miss him. And I miss the farm. I used to sit and watch you work, Lizzy. My land, I never saw any mortal creature work so hard in my life. When I first came to live with you and Lewis, I'd forgotten how hard you always worked at home, and I felt so bad for you, up at God knows when to milk the cow, and you never stopped moving all day, banging and clattering and clanging pots and pans around, rattling all over the house, out to plant flowers and pick peas. My God, I thought, this woman is going to screw herself right into the floorboards. And Lewis just let you work, he never tried to stop you. At first I thought he was taking advantage of you, but after a while I understood — that's what made you happy, you always had to be doing something for somebody, getting something done, and Lewis knew it, and he loved you for it, and he was smart enough to let you alone while you did it. It must be so awful for you to just lay in that bed day after day. I hardly ever come to see you any more because it makes me feel so bad, because I still have my life. I've got my piano and my cat, such as he is, and my rocker, and Monday Night Football, in season, and the newspaper. But you've lost your life. And there's not a thing I can do about it. I can't even tell you what I think about it. I try, but all that comes out is AAAAAAAAAAh. But I wouldn't trade what I have, not for anything. I can hear the music, in my head, I hear it. Probably when I play it doesn't sound to you much like what's in my head any more, the fingers gradually get used to landing on the wrong places, I expect, but what I hear in my head hasn't changed, you see, from when I used to play it right, when I was a little girl, before the fever came and took away the sound. The farm is in my head too now, so I can take it up to Molly's with me and never lose it. But I don't think you work that way, Lizzy, and I don't know how to comfort you. Maybe I could play you a song. Would you like that? Do you know what my dream is, Lizzy? My dream is that some day some magical transformation would occur, some extraordinary event, and just once, Lizzy, just once I could play my waltz for you and Molly, and you could hear it the way I hear it in my head, not all out of tune on the wrong notes, but perfect. Every note perfect, and beautiful and just right. Just for you. That's my dream . . . However. I would also like to look like Greta Garbo, sing like Caruso, and dance like Nijinsky, but I take what I can get. I take what I can get.

ORANGE FLOWER WATER
Craig Wright

Dramatic

In this monologue, Beth, a woman in her thirties, is talking to the wife of the man with whom she has been having an affair. The two women are watching a kids' soccer game.

BETH: *(Absently, with an eye on the soccer game.)* When I was really little, you know, I thought God was like my Dad, only bigger. And, uh, just like it felt to walk through our house where my Dad had built all the furniture, that's how it felt to walk through the whole world. Everything seemed like it has a little note taped to it: "Thought you might like this tree!" "Thought you might like this sunset!" "Thought you might like this cute boy! I made him just for you!" You know what I mean? . . .

I told my guidance counselor in high school, you won't believe this, I told her I didn't need to choose a career, because God had a plan for my life. But she said she was part of how God let people *in* on His plans. And I believed her. And *that* was the beginning of the end . . . because after that, it was so easy to see everything that way. Making out in the back of Jeff Kostermnople's VW Bus seemed like God's way of letting me *in* on something; and drinking too much in college was God's way of letting me *in* on something. And now, just when I would really love to look out over those trees, Cathy, and see a little note: "Hi, Beth! Thought you might like this world" — I look around and there are no notes on anything, anywhere. *(After a beat.)* Cathy, I'm really sorry about what's happened. If it ever felt like a choice, I'd have chosen differently, but it never did. I'm sorry.

OTHER PEOPLE
Christopher Shinn

Dramatic

> *Petra, mid-twenties, is a poet and a stripper. Here, she is talking to an*
> *older man, with whom she is having dinner in a restaurant.*

PETRA: Okay. Okay. I'm a freshman in college. A dorm, like a prison, falling apart, roaches, like rats in a lab we are, okay? My roommate is — Dominican or something — and one night she makes this big greasy pot of fish, in this very greasy yellow sauce, and she leaves it simmering on the stove. She goes out to meet her boyfriend. I go into the kitchen. I open the pot. Me. And it looks like sewage. A huge — ridiculous this pot is. And I take out a spoon and think: I'll try this. And I do. I take another bite. Another. And I know, I am a rational being, I know she's cooked this for her boyfriend, they'll be back soon: the whole pot. All of it. And I run into the bathroom and I sit there I'm numb I put my hand into my mouth, okay? And I'm covered there in — fish — covered — I look — a ghoul — green, literally — and I'm thinking: *What?* Because I know enough to know this is not normal or healthy in any way and I want to know: *Why?* Why would I have done this: Why do I feel this way? What in the world — literally, what in the world in which I find myself living, what at this point in history, what could make a person feel this unbearable sadness and think these terrible thoughts? These thoughts: *I will never be loved. I cannot live in this world.* You see? Because — because my roommate is going to come home and say "Where is the fish" and the only answer is "Petra ate it." Petra ate the fish. And how can I go on? How can I go on without — and I know — that there are people who do not ask this question — because to know — is too much. Because society does not *afford* them the opportunity to know, and. Because they are in a constant state of *desire,* and desire, *want,* inhibits consciousness. To become conscious you must stifle yourself, resist your impulses. Not that I had this language then. But I knew; I decided. I decided next time I would not eat the fish. No matter what. No matter what pain that caused me I would put the fork down and place the lid on the pot and . . . *(Pause.)*

OTHER PEOPLE
Christopher Shinn

Dramatic

Petra, mid-twenties, is a poet and stripper. Here, she has come to the apartment of an older man with whom she has dined.

PETRA: You know what people want? I'll tell you, you, me, Quentin Tarantino, Bill Clinton, whether they know it or not, I'll tell you exactly what people want: love. As stupid as that sounds. . . . No, we're all the same, in this, in just this one way, look, look: They have on videotape of, they have children, they did this in Britain, this study, okay, and little kids would get beaten up by their mothers, little, two, and three years old, slapped, punched, disgusting — but when the nurse came into the room — they actually did this, secret videotape — when the nurse came in to stop the beating and take the baby from the abusive mother, the baby cried, the baby cried and tried to hang on to its mother. So. So whatever you want to call it, that's — the baby wants — love — so the love is inappropriate, so what, it's what the baby knows. . . .

I'm not drunk. Okay. You asked me once, you said are you in pain? And I lied. I said no. And I'm in pain because I am not loved. You see. And artists — there's so little love to go around — the promise of love is so fleeting and inconsistent so to get noticed — people do — what they *do* is — just like you cheated on your wife, you see it in art too, the terror of not being loved, safe art, meaningless art, pandering art, commercial art, titillating art, outrageous art, can we sell it, can I sell myself, will I be rewarded with money, with prestige, with recognition — all those things which are, which are *perversions* of love — and let me tell you. If there were more love to go around. And more consciousness and less fear. People might make beautiful things. Beautiful things. What are all these horrible disgusting movies with violence and anger and, you know, I mean, they're cries for help! You look at a Quentin Tarantino movie, you know, this man has never been loved. He has had no experience of love in his life. Art, the art can never be better than the person who made it.

REMBRANDT'S GIFT
Tina Howe

Dramatic

> *Polly is a photographer in her sixties whose lifework has been to photo-
> graphically document her own body. Here, she is talking to her husband,
> Walter.*

POLLY: I've been documenting *my* body for over forty years now. *(Embarrassed by her candor.)* Who said that? . . .

 It wasn't out of vanity, I assure you . . . Oh, I was attractive
enough, but hardly a beauty. . .

 I just got really curious as I started maturing into a . . . you
know . . . *woman.* I'd always been this scrawny tomboy when suddenly these . . . *breasts* started to bloom. *(Handling them.)* It was as-
tonishing! I mean, what were the chances? It was inevitable, of course,
I just never imagined it would happen to *me* . . . You know, like falling
in love or getting married . . . They were a total surprise. When I got
in the shower, I couldn't keep my hands off them! They were so soft,
yet firm . . . *(Handling them.)* So I took to striking dramatic poses to
show them off. *(Doing it.)* Raising my arms over my head, clasping
my hands behind my back, arching over the back of a chair, getting
down on all fours. . . .

 I was staggered! I couldn't believe they belonged to me! So I got
a camera and taught myself the rudiments of photography. Looking
back on it, I was incredibly resourceful, managing to turn my closet
into a makeshift dark room . . . I was barely fifteen, but desperate to
document this . . . *metamorphosis!* Isn't that why we pick up a camera or paintbrush in the first place? To fathom a mystery? The artistry
and control come later . . . If you're lucky. There were plenty of guys
doing female nudes — Steiglitz, Bill Brandt, and Edward Weston —
but who better than a woman to celebrate her own coming of age?
And by the same token — her inevitable disintegration?

SAVED OR DESTROYED
Harry Kondoleon

Comic

> *Lucille, a woman in her thirties to forties, is in bed with her husband, Maury, who wants to watch TV or read the Bible. They have just been to a party with another couple, whose relationship if quite different from theirs.*

LUCILLE: Cut the sound on that. . . . Here, give me that, I'll manipulate it. Did you think it was strange and not nice that they left so soon? I did. Mostly not nice. I'm not sorry. I don't miss them, except maybe Karin. I like Karin. Karin and Vinnie spent a lot of time together. That's nice. They like books. They read to each other out loud. Why are you reading the Bible now instead of listening to me? You're always reading the Bible. What's so interesting in there once you have read it once? I'm getting a little fed up with you, you know, Maury? You space out and you blabber. People have remarked on it. You're out of it. *(Wistful.)* This was supposed to be a nice summer, a summer to remember. We got a nice rental, more than we could afford, but with your brother paying two-thirds, affordable. Right near the nice beach. All the clean-cut college kids. I'd hoped it would be good for Vincent and for Karin, meeting new lively people and making contacts for when they go to college. But they just stayed alone together. Maybe they'll get married. They're not real cousins so maybe they'll get married and have children That wouldn't throw me, would it throw you? Maurice, in the name of the Virgin Mary and all her many martyrs, put down that Bible!

SELF DEFENSE
Carson Kreitzer

Dramatic

> *This extraordinary play is based on the true story of a Florida prostitute who murdered several of her customers before the police finally caught her. In this monologue Jo, the central character (thirties to forties), is talking to Lu, her girlfriend.*

JO: *(A low, insistent whisper.)* Honey, I

I killed a man today. I just gotta . . . I gotta talk through this a little bit. I know it upsets you an' I understand that. Christ, don't I spend my whole life tryin' to keep you clean from all this shit. Keep it away from you. Keep it from touching you. But this is . . . this is too much.

Today . . . Out in the woods. I had to make the choice. Him or me. I mean, part of it was instinct, a big part a how I managed it. You just . . . when you have to. When you know you're gonna die if you don't get this right. But for the instinct to kick in, I had to . . . I don't know how to explain it. Empty myself out. Of the fear, the attitude of, I'm a worthless piece a shit an this was gonna happen sooner or later. I had to turn my brain to thinking No, fuck this. I am not gonna die here. I had to decide that.

Shit, I'm so stupid sometimes. Thinkin' I can trust people. If they seem nice an' all. Cos he, you know, he seemed . . . but that was Bullshit. All parta this plan, get me into the woods get me away from where anybody might hear, might happen by. An he, shit, I'm tellin' you he had this thing planned out. It was . . . I never been so fuckin' scared. Not in a while. I thought those days were over, me gettin' inta cars like a fuckin' teenager, thinks they're invincible. That's why I just been stickin' to my regulars, years now. I told you that.

But I know. You gotta have your things. An the cable TV. I know, sweetie, you get bored when I'm not here during the day. I know. I

64

know I gotta take care a you. An don't you worry, I'm gonna do it. I'll just . . . keep my eye out. Watch myself.

Cos I swear, honey, I thought I wasn't gonna make it back to you today.

That's what I thought.

(A light snore from Lu.)

Look like an angel when you're asleep, I swear it. An angel.

I'll take care a you. Always.

Don't know what I'd ever do without you.

Baby.

SELF DEFENSE
Carson Kreitzer

Dramatic

> *This character is a Florida coroner who could be any age or sex. In the original production, the Coroner was played by the same actress who played Pandora, so I have included this in the women's monologue book. Self Defense is based on the true story of a Florida prostitute who murdered several of her customers. The police are very concerned about these murders. They couldn't care less about the many gruesome murders of prostitutes that have gone unsolved.*

CORONER: I've seen a lot of dead prostitutes, in my line of work. A lot. And it's not supposed to be something you get upset about. I am a doctor, after all. A doctor of the dead. And it's like cancer or something, as a doctor, you're not supposed to get upset about it. Curse God or — You're supposed to speak in calm, rational terms. Not alarm the patient. Comfort the family.

A coroner's main job is to listen.

Find out how this thing happened. Make the call.

Natural causes. Suicide. Homicide.

And these girls who come in, ripped up some of 'em in ways that speak of a hatred I can barely begin to comprehend.

I've been listening to their bodies. For years. Listening to stories of desecrations of the human body not to mention the spirit that I can only call evil. Although I never had much of a dialogue with God or any sort of metaphysical thing. Suddenly I am forced to have this conception of evil. This knowledge.

The listening — adds up. Sometimes I feel it is eroding me, like a high whistling wind over sandstone. I am becoming . . . mute and rough and rounded.

I didn't come to this job with any fancy ideas about justice. The

. . . orderliness appealed to me. The ability to find truths. Add detail upon detail, layering to conclusion.

Without too many people cluttering things up, if you want to know the truth. I . . . have a little trouble dealing with people. Figured I could do my job, do it well, have a large degree of privacy in my life. These things are important to me.

The ideas about justice — started springing up at me. After the bodies had been piling up. For a while. Girls, women, who should not have been on my table. Sure, I get some ODs, suicides, but it's the others. The ones who shouldn't have been on my table for another forty years. Who should never have gone through what they went through to get to my table. And they're whispering to me — Unsolved. Unsolved. Unsolved. Unsolved.

SELF DEFENSE
Carson Kreitzer

Dramatic

> *Daytona is an "exotic dancer" and prostitute. She could be anywhere from twenty-five to forty-five. Here, she is being interviewed by the police, who are trying to solve a series of murders.*

DAYTONA: Yeah, he gave me that TV and the VCR. Didn't have the three hundred in cash. Hooked 'em up for me and everything.

You ask me how I feel, how do I feel about him bein' dead. Well, it's weird anybody you knew even a little bit winds up dead. So I feel bad. But you know what? I'm not surprised.

How about that. The kinda stuff he was into, the kinda *impulses* he was useta gettin' satisfied, I'm not surprised the man is dead.

So now it's my turn to be not surprised. Just like people are not surprised when one a my kind turns up dead. Cops, people. Not unless it's college students, oh a nice girl got her fuckin' head cut off, then everybody's surprised. Everybody's up in arms, doing shit. Mobilizing special police task forces. Yeah, maybe if I was a college co-ed somebody'd give a shit if I wound up dead. Somebody'd try and figure out how it happened.

But I ain't no fuckin' college girl. My body winds up in a ditch, they're not gonna waste too much of a day on it. And whoever it was that decided I didn't count and no one would give a shit if he dumped me out by the side of I-95, whoever it was driving the last car I got into, he's hangin' around going to the grocery store, playing with his fuckin' kids maybe, watching the five-second blip about it on the evening news and probably none the worse for wear.

He had, that Waldren guy I'm talking about now, had what you call bad impulse control. So usedta throwin' around money, acting like a big man. I mean, this is the kind of guy wants what he wants. If he doesn't have the three hundred in cash, he'll go open up his repair shop and give you somebody's TV and VCR they're probably waiting to have fixed. Tell them there's been a break-in or some shit, I don't know. I mean, he never hurt me, but those things are tricky. You never know what's gonna set somebody off.

So, yeah, I'm not surprised Mr. Waldren met with an untimely death. I feel bad for the guy, but I'm not surprised.

SOMEPLACE WARM
Peter Macklin

Dramatic

Marie (thirty-one) is talking to her mother, Claire, about how she got pregnant. She was raped.

MARIE: Raped mother. I was raped . . . Oh, mom. Oh, mom. . . .
I was walking home. I was walking home. It was cold. I was walking home. And he came up from behind. It was late. Three thirty-six AM. Melissa's party. I was walking home and I felt cold metal nudged in my side and then a hand went over my face. I was walking home and he brought me into his apartment. I had no choice. I had no choice. His place was spotless. So clean. I looked up and it was him. It was the guy from the neighborhood. I saw him almost every day. We said hi to each other. He was even handsome. All I wanted was to get back home. He told me things. Told me that he couldn't help himself. He kept apologizing. "I'm sorry, I'm sorry." I just wanted to get back home. I managed to let out one scream. One scream. There was something in its timbre. I heard it when I let it out. Like when daddy killed that deer. I sounded like that deer. All I wanted was to get back home. A neighbor heard. He had heard my deer scream. He called the police because he heard a tussle in the hallway also. All I wanted was to get back home. He finished. It was done. He said he was sorry. He kept apologizing. I just wanted to go home. He never let go of that gun. He never did. There was silence. He paced back and forth. The door got knocked down. It was the police. They saw he had a gun and they shot him. Killed him. They told me that he had a previous record and that's why they knocked the door down. They brought me to the hospital. But I just wanted to get back home. . . .
But I'm fine now. I am. I wouldn't keep the baby if he were still alive. I know that.

SOMEPLACE WARM
Peter Macklin

Dramatic

Claire, fifty-one, is talking to her daughter, Marie, whom she has driven a long distance to see.

CLAIRE: Please open the door. It smells like pee out here. . . . I'm your mother, for pity's sake. Please. You must still . . . Please. *(Marie opens the door. Claire walks in. Silence. Silence.)* This was probably the wrong thing to do. *(Starts to the door.)* I'm sorry. *(Stops at the door.)* It's just that I drove all the way from Ohio to be here. For someone who doesn't drive a lot, that's a long trip. But what could I do? I sure wasn't going to fly. That is the most unnatural way to travel. To be crammed in a metal can and projected three miles up in the air? No thank you. I'll tell you. All those plane crashes you see on the evening news. It's just creepy. But I guess anything on the evening news is creepy. They have a way of making you scared to even wake up in the morning. Why can't they have a news channel that only reports good things? The world would be a much better place. But that's not the way things go. It just seems to be too much at times. *(Noticing the bag she's holding.)* You know, on my way here, I stopped at, oh, about twenty-five McDonald's and such. I'm surprised I'm not three hundred pounds by now. Anyway, I stopped at so many because I tried to talk myself out of coming at each one. I couldn't when I was driving because I seem to go into a trance when I drive. But I would stop and try to tell myself not to come, that you probably don't want to see me. So I found myself at these McDonalds ordering the same thing, the Kid's Meal. Why? I don't know. I could say it was because I wanted to watch what I ate but then I would have ordered one of them salads, you know? I wouldn't have eaten the dressing though. I've heard the dressing is more fattening than the burgers. But I didn't eat a salad. I just kept on eating those Kid's Meals. I told the workers that my grandkid was waiting for me. I see now, looking at you, that glow, that I was right but they knew I didn't really know for sure. I could see it in their faces. This one teenage girl stared at me like I was crazy. She reminded me of you when you were that age. Who gave her the right to judge me? Just because she was on the other side of that counter! Freckles. Bouncy. Like she knew everything. *(Pause.)* I hate to lie. But I was embarrassed! But these meals. They were so cute. The little burgers, like an angel made them. The little fries, like they were made only for kids. And the little drink. Every time I thought I was going to order the, let's say Double Quarter Pounder with Extra Cheese, I would just come out and say "Kid's Meal, please." I took it as a sign. From God. That I should keep on going. Here. I found my determination from those meals. So, I have toys. Lots of Kid's Meal toys. I would like to give them to you. I drove all the way from Ohio to give them to you. Highway to highway. Turnpike to turnpike. To here. I was just trying to be thoughtful. Listen to me ramble. I know. I don't want to cause trouble. Please, *please*, take these toys. Maybe the baby would like them. You could tell the baby they're from it's Grandma.

SORROWS AND REJOICINGS
Athol Fugard

Dramatic

> *Marta, a black South African woman, has been for many years the house-keeper of a famous poet named Dawid Olivier. She was also his lover. Here, she is talking to Allison, Dawid's wife, with whom he lived in England in exile, about the now-deceased man they both loved. Marta and Allison are both in their forties.*

MARTA: It was late at night. He had driven all around the location trying to find me. I still don't know how he managed to get this far. I didn't recognize him at first. He looked like a ghost standing there in the darkness. What does this old white man want, I thought to myself. But then: "Marta Barends," the way only he could say it. Anyway . . . I got dressed quickly and we came back down here. I opened the house — I've had his room ready and waiting for him all these years — and that is where he stayed until the end. . . .

He never went out . . .

No not even to see his oupa's grave. I tried to tell him it was his . . . his plig . . . his . . . his duty, but he just shook his head. He already knew he was going to be lying there with his oupa in a few weeks time. Didn't want to see nobody. Not even Mr. Bosman. But he spent a lot of time at the windows looking out . . . the street, the orchard at the back, and the mountains. One time I found him at the window in the little side bedroom. You know the one? You can see the trading store from there. He made me stand there with him and tell him all about the people coming and going out of the shop. Even the little children carrying their empty bottles for paraffin. He wanted to know their names and who their mommies and daddies was. Ate nothing. Just about said nothing.

I tried to make him tell me about London but he said there was nothing to tell. I felt so useless, sitting there in the bedroom with him. I could see he was sick and in pain but all he wanted me to do was tell him about the village and all the things what had happened since he was gone. And not just the important things like who got married and who had a baby and who was dead and so on, but any old rubbish that came into my head.

Like one day he asked me to tell him all the things that were on the shelves in the trading store — you know, the tins of pilchards, the packets of mealie-meal and sugar, the bottles of methylated spirit, Five Roses Tea, Koo Apricot Jam — and how much they cost. And he just lay there listening to me very hard as if I was telling him something important. And always in Afrikaans. I had to speak to him all the time in Afrikaans. *(Helpless gesture.)* I didn't know what else to do for him, what he really wanted. I knew by then he was dying, but all I could do was sit and watch.

SORROWS AND REJOICINGS
Athol Fugard

Dramatic

Rebecca is an eighteen-year-old South African girl, of mixed-race parent-age. She has not spoken for most of the play. Finally, she too begins to talk about her father, a white South African poet named Dawid Olivier. Here, she is talking to her mother, Marta, who was Dawid's housekeeper and lover.

Rebecca: *(Finally breaking her silence.)* He did, Mommy! *(Pause.)* He saw his daughter. . . .

He saw me. In here. The night before he died. . . .

I came here. Every day since he came back I've been wanting to come here and stand in front of him . . . but not with forgiveness in my heart. I wanted to tell him what he had done to you, Mommy. I wanted to tell him how much you have wasted your life waiting for him — sweeping and dusting and cleaning in here every day as if he was coming back tomorrow. I wanted to tell him that his beautiful stinkwood table wasn't shining from the Cobra wax polish, but from the tears you rubbed into it. I'm not talking about poetry. Real tears. Yours. I saw them in your eyes. I saw them run down your cheeks and splash on the table when you was polishing and talking to him.

Ja, do you know you do that? Talk to him as if he was here in the room with you? I've heard you — many times — when you thought you was alone in here. You tell me there are ghosts in here . . . well I believe you and you know why? Because I've seen one. You! That's what you've become . . . the ghost of a stinkwood servant look-ing after her dead masters and madams.

And I wanted to tell him that I was praying for the day when he would be gone so that the house could be sold and then some other

75

white family's "Stinkwood Marta" could come and start polishing the table. And who knows, if she's lucky maybe one day that white "master" will notice that she's got nice legs and tits and fuck her and another little bastard with light skin and straight hair will be born for everybody to point at and whisper about . . . because that, Mr. Dawid Olivier, was your only contribution to the new South Africa, Mr. Dawid Olivier . . . 'n spook kind *(Afrikaans.)*, a freak . . . and she is standing here in front of you. *(Pause.)*

That's why I came here that night. I knew you were here in the house, Mommy, and I wanted to say those things in front of you so that you could hear them as well. That way you would maybe wake up and see what he has done to you.

SORROWS AND REJOICINGS
Athol Fugard

Dramatic

Allison, a white woman in her forties, was married to Dawid Olivier, a white South African poet who died in exile in England. She has returned to South Africa for his funeral, where she learns that her husband has a child, Rebecca, with his black housekeeper, Marta, to both of whom she is speaking here.

ALLISON: *(Bitterly.)* "The Fires of South Africa"! Amazing! That was going to be the title of a poem he tried to write in London. We had just watched a BBC program about the township riots. Houses and buildings burning, barricades in the street, uniforms and guns and those hideous armored cars everywhere, a pall of tear gas and smoke over everything. It ended, as it always does, with the image of a woman weeping.

(She tries to remember the poem.) I think it went:

Fires of sorrow,

Fires of hate . . .

(Pause.) And then something like:

Incendiary tears

Ignite our fate . . .

I'll look for it when I get back and go through his papers. There might be a few other things that I can pull together to make a small volume, but I certainly won't be calling it *Rejoicings*.

I must go and pack. When you are finished in here, Marta, come past the guest house and I will give you that copy of Dawid's will.

(Allison starts to leave. At the entrance to the passageway she stops, turns back and speaks to Rebecca.)

For your soul's sake, Rebecca, I hope you know that what you did was terribly wrong. What you turned to ash and smoke out there in the veld was evidence of a man's love, for his country, for his people — for you! Don't reject it. That love was clean and clear and good! It was the best of him. For your soul's sake claim it, Rebecca. Rejoice in it! Because if you think you and your "new South Africa" don't need it, you are making a terrible mistake. You are going to need all the love you can get, no matter where it comes from.

THE THEORY OF EVERYTHING
Prince Gomolvilas

Comic

> *Patty is an Asian-American woman in her late thirties, part of a group of people who gather atop a Las Vegas wedding chapel every week for a UFO watch. She is obsessed with UFOs. Note: Although this monologue was originally conceived to be played by an Asian-American, for your use in class or auditions you don't necessarily have to be Asian-American.*

> *Patty stands, facing the audience.*

PATTY: I want to talk about aliens. Not people from other countries. I want to talk about space creatures. Those types of aliens. You know what I'm talking about: big head, big black eyes, tiny holes where the nose should be, extremely thin lips. They fly around in large metallic ships covered with bright lights, and they abduct normal human beings like you and me.

I read that the chances of a person seeing a UFO is equal to the chances of a person witnessing a bank robbery.

I'm thirty-nine, and I have never seen a UFO. But I have witnessed *five* bank robberies.

I am *way* overdue for a Close Encounter. I mean, just look at the odds.

Sometimes when I watch reruns of *The X-Files* and see all these amazing things happening to ordinary people — to ordinary white people — I get angry. Jealous, maybe. When is it going to be my turn? Can't life be fair for once? I deserve to see a UFO. I deserve to be abducted by aliens. I've been waiting so long for *something* to happen. *This* is my something, and I want it now.

So here's what I've figured out: They're not going to come to me until I've shown them that I'm ready. I think that they think that I've been unprepared.

But no longer, I rent videos, read books, watch documentaries, do research at the library. I've taken in an enormous amount of information on the subject. I know everything there is to know about Area 51, about Project Blue Book, about Roswell. I've written letters to the president, to my congressman, to the military, to NASA and to David Duchovny.

What do they say?

"Be Prepared."

Well, guess what?

I *am*.

(Blackout.)

TRANSATLANTIC
Judy Klass

Seriocomic

Fiona is an English woman, high-strung, educated, brilliant, and beautiful, who needs American money to get her screenplay produced, but she is not pleased about it. She finds America and Americans fairly revolting, dreads how they will change her script, and sees their input as tantamount to cultural imperialism. Yet she and her quiet banker husband Nick are having Bernie Greenfield, an indie film producer from New York, and his wife Lori over for dinner at their London home; Fiona is talking to Nick in their bedroom, getting ready, as she speaks these words:

FIONA: What's the time? *(Nervous, mustering.)* Oh, bloody marvelous. And I can't even find a pair of earrings to match this . . . I'm not trying to look lovely. I'm trying to look like a flashy corporate wheeler-dealer. Something this fellow will respect. Am I overdressing? Do you suppose he'll turn up in trainers and a torn sweatshirt, with five-day stubble and a little ponytail at the back? What is the matter with my hair? It's frightful!

(Snapping.) No! We can't put it off, they'll suppose we're incompetent, what do you think? Just sit tight. *(Beat.)*

Oh, I'm sorry, Nick, I'm a mess. Don't mind me. I'm counting on you, you know that. You've got to save me from myself. You mustn't let me say an honest word this whole grisly evening . . . Yes, we'll have to show them where all the McDonalds are, and take them to the Guinness Book of Records Museum.

(Fake Yank accent.) "Gee, this is a great little country you got here, honey. Think I'll buy it." *(A beat.)*

Like them? Not a chance. I know what type he is from our chats on the phone. He's all charm, and bluff good fellowship. He'll have a handshake that'll crush every bone in your fingers, wait and see.

I've no idea what she's like. Probably some ghastly, cosmetically altered little trollop.

If they're in the film industry they'll ooze Hollywood wherever they live, trust me.

(Bitterly, with fake Yank accent.) No, you're right, we gotta think positive. We're gonna bond with these swell people. They're our new best friends!

(She throws an earring down in disgust, chooses another pair, and speaks normally.)

It's ironic, actually. Here I've been a good girl, toadying up to the men in the company, and finally I get a chance to produce my film, with my script — and I've got to impress some Yank bastard, and sell my soul to coax money out of him. It makes perfect sense.

(Incredulous.) Yes, dear, that's right, he said I'll retain creative control — which means precisely nothing. They come up with that sort of jargon to fill up their contracts to keep their five million lawyers per square inch employed, when they're not suing each other. But if his company puts up more than half the funds, you can bet they'll have their sweaty little hands all over the film.

(Stopped short.)

Why should it surprise you he's interested?

(Defensive.) Oh yes, it's going to be a colossal flop, isn't it? Who would want to see a film about John Stuart Mill and Harriet Taylor? How snoringly dull! No, you're right, of course. It's not their sort of thing at all. Mill was an intellect, and American culture is all about celebrating stupidity, just switch on Jerry Springer. I should know, I have to read their cinema trade papers.

(She yanks a comb through her hair as she says each name.)

Wayne's World. Dumb and Dumber. Hot Chick. Old School. And the apotheosis *Forrest Gump.* No wonder they loved Reagan so much, or "W." They see an intelligent script and they don't know what to do with it — any more than they know what to do with an intelligent president who can talk in complete sentences.

(Fiona swigs her wine. When she says "Bernard," she pronounces it the British way: BUH-nud. When she quotes him, she lapses into a fake American accent again.)

82

Well, according to our good friend Bernard, WaveLine Productions is a young "highbrow, alternative" company, looking for "arty, intellectual projects." So, just imagine what "arty" suggestions he'll make to enhance my script. A bit of shagging, of course.

(Fake accent.) Can't have a sexless marriage, lady. What we got here is boy meets girl, boy is impotent, girl is frigid — but they get over it! They go on to have wild, crazy, Technicolor sex!

(Her normal accent.) Violence? In the life of Mill? That's a difficult proposition, let's see — Oh, I know!

(With fake accent.) — Okay, here's the pitch. Mill goes down the pub — goes into a bar, see? And there's Carlyle. And Mill says, Tom, I'm an abolitionist, ya wanna make something of it? And Carlyle says, yeah, John, I think the wogs on the Jamaican plantations should stay slaves. So Mill pops him one — whammo! — right in the kisser. Now that's a movie! Plus a car chase scene. A bit of MTV flash editing, a throbbing title track by Bryan Adams . . .

(Sadly.) Enjoy it? Yes, you would do, wouldn't you. Are you sure you don't want to ask Sharon to stay and serve?

(Beat.) If he introduces me to his inner child, I'll molest it on the spot, I swear to God I will!

TRANSATLANTIC
Judy Klass

Seriocomic

Lori Greenfield is speaking to Nick, a mild English banker, in the guest bedroom of the London home belonging to Nick and his wife Fiona. Lori's husband Bernie and Fiona are downstairs arguing about possible changes in a film script that Fiona wrote and that Bernie's company wants to produce. Originally, the Greenfields were dinner guests, but arguments and various awkward moments were sinking the project, and to save it, Nick suggested the Greenfields spend the night. Lori and Nick have been mostly quiet while the two couples were together; each seeks to support his or her more colorful and confident spouse. Bernie has humiliated Lori before their hosts several times in the course of the evening and now, just before Lori speaks, Nick has cautiously remarked on it:

LORI: *(Speaking rapidly.)* It's okay. Bernie's just nervous. He, like, wants to impress you guys so bad — and I keep embarrassing him. I'm so "Westchestuh." And I babble. I can't help it, even when I know I'm doing it . . . No, I'm a babbler. That's always my problem. And Bernie's so smart. He's turned me on to so many ideas, so many good books, Nick — I wish I could tell you. I learn a lot just being around him. It's hard to understand him sometimes. I've known him for ages, so it's easier for me. We've just been married three years, but I had a big crush on him in high school. I was too shy to even talk to him. Then years later, I saw him at my cousin Craig's bar mitzvah, back in Westchester. I'd heard that he went to Princeton and won the Rhodes and all. But I saw him, and I thought: This time I'm gonna say something. This time I won't let him get away . . . Yeah, well, we lived together for a long time. I was surprised he was interested in me — but, you know, Bernie's kind of a lonely guy. He's got all these defense systems. I was getting my degree in child psychology, and he didn't think it was so funny back then. He was real supportive. Bernie puts up with a lot from me. 'Cause, like, I've got all these problems, like bulimia sometimes. And plus, I can be a little neurotic-compulsive, and I get insomnia when I'm alone . . .Yeah, I felt terrible about Princess Diana. It was such a shame. She was such a beautiful person. And those two kids . . . Bernie made fun of me for staying up all night to watch the funeral. But I remember, when I first moved in with him, and she was getting divorced, and the papers kept saying how unhappy she was and all? And her lousy marriage, and how she kept trying to kill herself? I'd see the tabloid headlines, and I'd kind of identify with her — 'cause of the bulimia and all. And I thought, maybe it's a bad sign for my relationship that I'm so sad for Princess Di. But, y'know, I love Bernie so much. He just — makes me nuts when he goes into his Grand Rabbi of Westchester routine. He starts lecturing me, explaining stuff — and he just out-words me. I'm not in his league, let's face it. Plus, it's a weird marriage. Like, Bernie explained to me — he's not afraid of commitment. But he doesn't believe in monogamy — he thinks most marriages stifle both parties. So, we keep things open . . .

Why? I mean, technically, I'm free too. But after a long day, just want to curl up with him. I hope this trip will be good for us . . . Oh I love London! I'm so excited to be here! I've always loved British TV shows, and movies, and accents. It still doesn't seem real — you know, the money looks like Monopoly money. Bernie didn't want to take me, I practically begged him. I'm making him sound awful. It's just — he's so smart, and sometimes I can't keep up.

THE TRIAL OF ONE SHORT-SIGHTED BLACK WOMAN VS. MAMMY LOUISE AND SAFREETA MAE

Karani Marcia Leslie

Seriocomic

> *This stylized, wildly funny, and provocative satire uses the framework of a trial to explore the idea that if black people don't explore their own history, or if they persist in thinking that "reality" is what they see on film or TV, they will be unable to cope with what has become an increasingly complex and hostile world. Here, the Prosecution is speaking to us at the start of the trial, as if we were the jury. She is old enough to have passed the bar, and old enough to "remember when."*

PROSECUTION: Ladies and gentlemen of the courtroom. You are our jury. You are about to embark on a serious dialogue, a dialogue that concerns images. Now, I ask you. When you think of the chief executive of a corporation, does a black woman come to mind? When you think of an airline pilot, do you think black woman? And if for any reason you should need heart surgery — and I pray you do not — do you say to yourself, I want a black woman? My point exactly. Black America is tired of the images that Mammy Louise and Safreeta Mae represent. . . .

My client lives in shame and humiliation. It is a constant torture that represses her dreams and her ability to communicate who she really is. My client is a black woman. A black woman who realizes that to be whole she must love and find beauty in herself; but who can hardly find such love or beauty because she has been taught throughout the history of these United States that no such beauty exists within a black woman. This black woman and countless others must constantly fight the insults and lack of respect that is forthcoming, not only from a white society but from within her community. The black woman is not held in high regard as reflected by a society that despises her children, but deems her sexuality as whorish and that pays her the lowest salary for the same contributions. She is a woman in disgrace, ladies and gentlemen. And I intend to prove that the defendants, Mammy Louise and Safreeta Mae did willfully conspire, with the major chroniclers of American history and the media, to place her in disgrace. That they did create the big fat laughing hyena of a Mammy and her hot-to-trot siren daughter to destroy my client's self-esteem and discourage society from delegating a high regard to any other black woman. And if I do my job well — which I intend to do — the defendants will be barred from appearing in and conspiring with any future TV or film productions, in any way, whether that be a remake of *Pinky* or Aunt Jemima with a perm!

THE TRIAL OF ONE SHORT-SIGHTED BLACK WOMAN VS. MAMMY LOUISE AND SAFREETA MAE

Karani Marcia Leslie

Dramatic

> *This stylized, wildly funny, and provocative satire uses the framework of a trial to explore the idea that if black people do not explore their own history, or if they persist in thinking that "reality" is what they see on film or TV, they will be unable to cope with what has become an increasingly complex and hostile world. Here the defense attorney, whose name is Zora, is speaking to Leroy, a bottom-line sort, a product of the 1980s "Greed is Good" era. She is in her forties to fifties, but she could be played by an actress of any age.*

DEFENSE: Thirty years old. The civil rights struggle was in full swing by the time you were born. I guess you don't remember it though. . . . Well I was there. One of the demands was to have representation on any level where it affects us. And film and television affects us. Well, we got it. Because here you sit. A black studio executive. Believing in his or her own merit. Well you're wrong to do that, Mr. Johnson. Because you didn't become an executive because you graduated from Harvard or Yale. You became an executive because somebody sat in, somebody marched, somebody got beat down, hosed down, jailed, and bit by dogs, so that when you did graduate from Harvard or Yale, you'd have somewhere to go. People gave their lives. Their lives, Mr. Johnson! They served your interest, Leroy. All we ask you to do is serve somebody else's besides your own! *(Pause.)* You see, I can understand fear. But I can't accept that you don't owe! Because you didn't exist before us! We loud-talking, head wrap–wearing, Daishiki-sportin' so-called Zula Boolas thought you up and made you a reality! You owe, Mr. Johnson! You owe! No further questions.

THE TRIAL OF ONE SHORT-SIGHTED BLACK WOMAN VS. MAMMY LOUISE AND SAFREETA MAE

Karani Marcia Leslie

Dramatic

This stylized, wildly funny, and provocative satire uses the framework of a trial to explore the idea that if black people do not explore their own history, or if they persist in thinking that "reality" is what they see on film or TV, they will be unable to cope with what has become an increasingly complex and hostile world. Here Victoria, a rather snooty, well-off woman in her thirties or forties, is testifying, in response to a question made by an attorney.

VICTORIA: Look, I started reading Terry McMillan's *Waiting to Exhale.* I could not relate to those women! And I did read a few pages of Toni Morrison's *Beloved* . . . and I've got to tell you . . . I couldn't understand it. I also flipped through Maya Angelou's inaugural poem. . . . I was in a fog again. Who are they writing for? Not me! And Alice Walker's *Colored Purple* — . . .

Whatever! I didn't read it! I saw the movie. And I didn't particularly care for that! I guess it's the subject matter — what they write about. It just doesn't interest me. . . .

What I mean is most black writers write about poor black people and the past. I don't want to read about poor black people and the past. And I don't want to read writers who write about the godly simplicity of the rural backwoods negro . . . or writers who try to turn poverty into some kind of sainthood — always emphasizing the integrity of the struggling ghetto black. Somebody's always got to be struggling. Then there are those writers who go on and on about the higher intelligence of the African. If they were so intelligent, they'd a been smart enough to keep the white man out of Africa. Not to mention the writers who try to rescue buffoons who can't even speak correct English from society's condemnation. And let's not talk about slavery? Cause I — HATE — SLAVERY!!! Why is everyone trying to find something noble in such a disgraceful condition. I want to be as far away from that part of history as I possibly can and from those women. Because *(Rising slowly and pointing.)* I hate them too. I hate everything, everything, every THING THEY REPRESENT!!!

U.S. DRAG
Gina Gionfriddo

Comic

Allison, a young woman in her twenties, is obsessed with coming up with a scheme to make as much money as fast as she can, with as little effort as possible.

ALLISON: I cried this morning. I was reading a book about JonBenet Ramsey. . . .

This girl who baby-sat her a few times got $5,000 from a magazine. The lady who cleaned her house got $20,000. These magazines wrote just enormous checks to anyone who ever knew her. *(Pause.)* It just seems like you can get a lot of money if you're in the right place when something really bad happens. Like that woman who went to the hospital for a Caesarean and got a crazy doctor who carved his initials in her belly. She got millions of dollars. Just for having a scar. I would have a scar. It just seems unfair. Monica Lewinsky got to go to the Oscars and she wasn't in any movies! I want to go to the Oscars! There are all these people who are not as good-looking and smart as me and they are getting money and getting on TV and they didn't do anything except be nearby when something bad happened. It isn't fair! It just isn't fair! I don't have any money and nobody knows who I am! I want to do nothing and get money and have people know who I am! *(Silence.)* I'm sorry. It just . . . came out of me. I'm sorry.

WHAT DIDN'T HAPPEN
Christopher Shinn

Seriocomic

Elaine is an actress in her early forties, visiting a novelist friend at his house in the country. She has just about had it with the acting profession.

ELAINE: I don't know . . . *(Elaine pauses, looks up at the sky as if struck by something.)* The last regional job I took. I did Hedda in Hartford. It was a respectful production but it wasn't a museum piece — it had life and spontaneity to it. Well. I got miserably depressed. Getting into that tight dress every night I thought — why do I have to wear this? I want to wear normal clothes. What the hell do I know about Hedda Gabler? It all began to feel vaguely humiliating. And I would walk around Hartford and think, I want to tell *that* story — that woman at the Dunkin' Donuts with three kids — Women who are alive today. So I came back to New York and I said, "That's it." Only new plays from now on . . . *(Pause.)*

They didn't cast me. The MFAs started pumping out pretty young things, new directors with new girlfriends came up. *(Beat.)* I got older. *(Beat.)* You know, what Dave does — novelists — they get "better" with age, they increase in esteem in society's eyes. No one tells Saul Bellow he's irrelevant. There's respect. What *I* do — the more I know, the less I matter. I'm finally old enough that I have something interesting to tell the world, and no one wants to hear it.

WHERE'S MY MONEY?
John Patrick Shanley

Dramatic

> *Celeste is an out-of-work actress in her twenties to thirties who's been
> cheating on her boyfriend with a married man. Here she is having a
> drink with Natalie, an old friend whom she hasn't seen in years.*

CELESTE: There's an atmosphere with this guy . . . of murder. He wouldn't
murder me — that's not what I'm saying — but it's there. Like an
aroma. I could smell this thing on him when we met. He was intro-
ducin' himself, sayin' hello, bein' nice. We're in a public place. I remember thinkin', he's going to rape me. And seeing like, police
photographs in my head. Of me. And right like that, right out of that,
I gave him my phone number. I walked away like there was a camera recording me and music I was walking to. And I felt like I was in
a ghost story about love. A week later, we meet up. I'm alone with
him for the first time. It's in his office. I walk in his office. He closes
the door. "Click." And I feel this weight come over my arms and legs.
I was scared. 'Cause he was goin' to do something to me. And I wanted
him to do something to me. I was afraid and I wanted to be afraid.
I wanted fear. I was tired of being "good girl." The first time I went
to him, I went to his office. I dressed all in white. Can you imagine?
Like a sacrifice. I had this book, *Return of the Native.* And I just started
talking about Eustacia Vye because I was so nervous. And he didn't
call me on it. He didn't say, "What are you talking about this book?
That's not what's going on here." He just talked back to me about
Eustacia Vye. But while he talked, he put his hand on the bone in
my chest, and he slowly pushed me down. He never stopped talking
about what I was talking about, but he was pushing and I was going
down. And then his hands and my whole anatomy went to this other
world and we did things without words. What we were saying was
like we were another bunch of people in a very different room. A room

without words. We had a secret from ourselves. There was a lot of blood. I got my period right in the middle . . . He's . . . He was big. I guess it knocked something loose. He hadda go out to a store and buy me a raincoat to put over myself. 'Cause, Natalie, I looked like I'd just been born. And this was in an office. This was in a man's office. In the middle of the day.

WHERE'S MY MONEY?
John Patrick Stanley

Comic

Natalie, an accountant in her twenties to thirties, is having a drink with Celeste, an out-of-work actress, an old friend whom she hasn't seen in a while. While Celeste is something of a dreamy, ditzy romantic, Natalie is no-nonsense, all business.

NATALIE: All right, I'll just lay it out for you. You're a whore. . . .

Don't. Please. It's hard enough without you playing surprised. Don't tell me you haven't thought about the fact that you're a whore. A STUPID whore. . . .

I'll break it down for you. First thing. The count. Let's do the count. You're thirty-one. Next year, you'll be guess what? Twenty-three? No. Thirty-two. And it goes on from there. Older, older, older. A flight of stairs going down, down, down. You're like a quart of milk reaching its expiration date. Have you ever tried to sell a pumpkin the day after Halloween? That's what you are facing. Are you ready? I don't think so. Is it just? Who cares. Pick a fight with God. See where you get. It's the truth of what it is to be a woman. . . .

France! Then go to France! Climb the Eiffel Tower. Feed the pigeons. Maybe they'll be glad to see you. Please! You're in America. Do the math. Next. You've gotta face the facts. You've got a birth defect. You've got a limp. How many parts are there for limping girls?

Laura in *The Glass Menagerie*. And that's it! Have there been any productions of that play? . . .

And did you get that part? . . .

Then it's time for you to stop office-temping and doing Romeo's girlfriend in acting class and get a bona fide fucking job. It's two plus two. You have to drop the lollipop and pick up the car keys! Next issue. Kenny. This may sound tough, but I'm going to say it anyway. Kenny's your best bet. . . .

Yes, he's a loser. But what are you at this point? Maybe together you can pull your car out of the ditch and make some miles down the road. I know where you're at, Celeste. There's a million women like you. You don't want to look at your story 'cause you don't like your story, so you just close your eyes and tell yourself a fucking fairy tale. And you know what that makes you? In a world of men? Totally exploitable. 'Cause you want the lie. You got no interest in the truth. What's the truth ever done for you? The truth of your life is like a bad magazine. Boring story, lousy pictures. Which brings me to your mysterious, exciting, cheeseball stud. Who smacks you around because he's afraid of his wife. Do I even have to talk about this rodent? A married violent scumbug who slips you a Saturday Night Special for what? Valentines Day? You can't look at what this guy pegged the minute he smelled that thrift-shop essential oil you use for perfume. You're a pushover. Is this your notebook? . . .

What have you been writing? . . .

Poetry. You're going down in flames. Unless you get it together, they are going to pass you around like chicken wings.

WHITEOUT
Alan Newton

Dramatic

> Whiteout *takes place in a remote cabin in Alabama, owned by Mark, who is hosting a holiday gathering of friends. During this reunion, a freak snowstorm occurs, and nobody can leave, so they begin talking about their pasts, together and apart. Cathy, a professor of English from Michigan, is here talking to Mark about the first day she met him.*

CATHY: Well, the first day of ninth grade, here I am, the strange new girl from Detroit, and my dad and I drive up in his little Yugo — the car that looked like a hemorrhoid! The first thing I hear as I'm walking to my brand-new school is some girl say, "Is that a car or a shoe box?" Later that day, somebody asked me, "Are you a girl or a boy?" but that's another story. Anyway, I suddenly just froze, right there in front of everyone. *(Stops moving.)* I couldn't move a toe. Have you ever dreamed that you're running somewhere, and you're late, but the harder you try to kick your legs, the slower you move? That's exactly how I felt, but I was wide awake. I was ten yards away from my new school, but I'd never felt farther away from anything. I turned back around to see if Dad was still there, and every car I saw was a Cutlass, a Beamer, or a Volvo station wagon. All the kids getting out of them were tall and tan and yearbook-cute, all the parents behind the wheels looked like tennis pros. . . . And then, lo and behold, into the lot comes the *only* car whose status was anywhere near that tenth circle of hell in which the Yugo will forever languish — . . . A 1977, burnt-orange, AMC Pacer — ! . . . And I knew I had a friend.

PERMISSION ACKNOWLEDGMENTS

ALL THINGS BEING EQUAL by Leonora B. Rianda Copyright 2000 by Lauren Friesen. Reprinted by permission of Dramatic Publishing, 311 Washington St., Woodstock, IL 60098, 815-338-7170 (ph), 815-338-8981 (fx). All rights reserved. The entire text of *All Things Being Equal* has been published by Dramatic Publishing in *Best Student One Acts, Vol. 4.*

ALTER EGOS by Jon McGovern Copyright 2000 by Lauren Friesen. Reprinted by permission of Dramatic Publishing, 311 Washington St., Woodstock, IL 60098, 815-338-7170 (ph), 815-338-8981 (fx). All rights reserved. The entire text of *Alter Egos* has been published by Dramatic Publishing in *Best Student One Acts, Vol. 4.*

APRIL by Alison Fields Copyright 2000 by Lauren Friesen. Reprinted by permission of Dramatic Publishing, 311 Washington St., Woodstock, IL 60098, 815-338-7170 (ph), 815-338-8981 (fx). All rights reserved. The entire text of *April* has been published by Dramatic Publishing in *Best Student One Acts, Vol. 4.*

AVOW by Bill C. Davis Copyright by 1999 by Bill C. Davis. Reprinted by permission of Susan Schulman, 454 W. 44th St., New York, NY 10036. All rights reserved. The entire text of *Avow* has been published in an acting edition by Dramatists Play Service, 440 Park Ave. S., New York, NY 10016, 212-MU3-8960 (ph), 212-213-1539 (fx). CAUTION: Professional and amateurs are hereby warned that *Avow* is subject to a royalty. The play is fully protected under the copyright laws of the United States of America, and of all countries covered by the International Copyright Union (including the Dominion of Canada and the rest of the British Commonwealth), and of all countries covered by the Pan-American Copyright Convention and the Universal Copyright Convention, and of all countries with which the United States has reciprocal copyright relations. All rights, including professional, amateur, motion picture, recitation, lecturing, public reading, radio broadcasting, television, video or sound taping, all other forms of mechanical or electronic reproductions such as information storage and retrieval systems and photocopying, and all rights of translation into foreign languages, are strictly reserved. All inquiries should be addressed to Susan Schulman: A Literary Agency, 454 West 44th St., New York, NY 10036, attn.: Susan Schulman. E-mail: Schulman@aol.com.

BANG by Laura Shaine Cunningham Copyright 2002 by Laura Shaine Cunningham. Reprinted by permission of Bruce Ostler, Bret Adams Ltd., 448 W. 44th St., New York, NY 10036. All rights reserved. The entire text of this play have been published by Broadway Play Publishing, 56 E. 81st St., New York, NY 10028-0202, 212-772-8354 (ph), 212-772-8358 (fx), in *Plays by Laura Shaine Cunningham.*

BEAUTIFUL BODIES by Laura Shaine Cunningham Copyright 2002 by Laura Shaine Cunningham. Reprinted by permission of Bruce Ostler, Bret Adams Ltd., 448 W. 44th St., New York, NY 10036. All rights reserved. The entire text of this play have been published by Broadway Play Publishing, 56 E. 81st St., New York, NY 10028-0202, 212-772-8354 (ph), 212-772-8358 (fx), in *Plays by Laura Shaine Cunningham.*

BINGO BABES by Isabel Duarte Copyright 2000, 2002 by Isabel Duarte. Reprinted by permission of Samuel French, Inc. (Attn.: Linda Kirland), 45 W. 25th St., New York, NY 10010. All rights reserved. The entire text of *Bingo Babes* has been published in an acting edition by Samuel French, Inc., 45 W. 25th St., New York, NY 10010, 212-206-8990 (ph), 212-206-1429 (fx).

BLACK SHEEP by Lee Blessing Copyright by Lee Blessing. Reprinted by permission of Judy Boals, Judy Boals, Inc., 208 W. 30th St., Suite 401, New York, NY 10001. All rights reserved. As of this printing the entire text of *Black Sheep* has not been published; but it will no doubt be published at some unspecified future date in an acting edition by Dramatists Play Service.

BLOWN SIDEWAYS THROUGH LIFE by Claudia Shear Copyright 2002 by Claudia Shear. Reprinted by permission of International Creative Management (Attn.: Mitch Douglas), 40 W. 57th St., New York, NY 10019. All rights reserved. The entire text of *Blown Sideways Through Life* (which, as a one-person monodrama, is crammed with great monologue material) has been published in an acting edition by Samuel French, Inc., 45 W. 25th St., New York, NY 10010, 212-206-8990 (ph), 212-206-1429 (fx).

BOOK OF DAYS by Lanford Wilson Copyright 2000 by Lanford Wilson. Reprinted by permission of Grove/Atlantic, Inc., 841 Broadway, New York, NY 10003. All rights reserved. The entire text of *Book of Days* has been published by Grove Press and will no doubt soon be available in an acting edition from Dramatists Play Service, 440 Park Ave. S., New York, NY 10016, 212-MU3-8960 (ph), 212-213-1539 (fx).

BOYS & GIRLS by Tom Donaghy Copyright 2002 by Tom Donaghy. Reprinted by permission of Sarah Jane Leigh, International Creative Management, 40 W. 47th St., New York, NY 10019. All rights reserved. The entire text of *Boys & Girls* has been published by Smith and Kraus, Inc. in *New Playwrights: The Best Plays of 2002.* By the time this book comes out, it will no doubt be published as well in an acting edition by Dramatists Play Service, 440 Park Ave. S., New York, NY 10016, 212-MU3-8960 (ph), 212-213-1539 (fx). CAUTION: *Boys & Girls,* being duly copyrighted is subject to a royalty. The North American stage performance rights (other than first class rights) are controlled by Dramatists Play Service, Inc. No professional or non-professional performance of the play (excluding first class professional performance) may be given without obtaining in advance the written permission of Dramatists Play Service Inc., and paying the requisite fee. Inquiries concerning all other rights should be addressed to Sarah Jane Leigh c/o ICM, 40 West 57th St., New York, NY 10019.

CONTROL FREAKS by Beth Henley Copyright 2002 by Beth Henley. Reprinted by permission of Peter Hagan, The Gersh Agency, 41 Madison Ave., New York, NY 10010. All rights reserved. The entire text of *Control Freaks* has been published in an acting edition by Dramatists Play Service, 440 Park Ave. S., New York, NY 10016, 212-MU3-8960 (ph), 212-213-1539 (fx).

CRUISING CLOSE TO CRAZY by Laura Shaine Cunningham Copyright 2002 by Laura

Shaine Cunningham. Reprinted by permission of Bruce Ostler, Bret Adams Ltd., 448 W. 44th St., New York, NY 10036. All rights reserved. The entire text of this play have been published by Broadway Play Publishing, 56 E. 81st St., New York, NY 10028-0202, 212-772-8354 (ph), 212-772-8358 (fx), in *Plays by Laura Shaine Cunningham.*

THE DEAD EYE BOY by Angus MacLachlan Copyright 2002 by Angus MacLachlan. Reprinted by permission of Peter Hagan, The Gersh Agency, 41 Madison Ave., New York, NY 10010. All rights reserved. The entire text of *The Dead Eye Boy* has been published in an acting edition by Dramatists Play Service, 440 Park Ave. S., New York, NY 10016, 212-MU3-8960 (ph), 212-213-1539 (fx).

THE DYING GAUL by Craig Lucas Copyright 2002 by Craig Lucas. Reprinted by permission of Peter Franklin, William Morris Agency, Inc., 1325 Ave. of the Americas, New York, NY 10019. All rights reserved. The entire text of *The Dying Gaul* has been published in an acting edition by Samuel French, Inc., 45 W. 25th St., New York, NY 10010, 212-206-8990 (ph), 212-206-1429 (fx).

FROZEN STARS by David Matthew Barnes Copyright by David Matthew Barnes. Reprinted by permission of the author. The entire text of *Frozen Stars* is published by Stage One Theatrical Publications, who may be contacted via their Web site (www.sotheatre.com) or via e-mail (sotheatre@aol.com).

GIVE ME YOUR ANSWER, DO! By Brian Friel Copyright 1997, 2000 by Brian Friel. Reprinted by permission of Jack Tantleff, William Morris Agency, Inc., 1325 Avenue of the Americas, New York, NY 10019. All rights reserved. The entire text of *Give Me Your Answer, Do!* has been published in an acting edition by Dramatists Play Service, 440 Park Ave. S., New York, NY 10016, 212-MU3-8960 (ph), 212-213-1539 (fx).

HOMECOMING by Lauren Weedman Copyright 2002 by Lauren Weedman. Reprinted by permission of the author. All rights reserved. All inquiries should be sent to Maryann Lombardi, Boulevard Artists, inc., 2373 Broadway, #1508, New York, NY 10019. The entire text of *Homecoming* has been published by Smith & Kraus, Inc. in *Women Playwrights: The Best Plays of 2002.* Note: Lotsa other good monologues therein.

JAR THE FLOOR by Cheryl L. West Copyright 2002 by Cheryl L. West. Reprinted by permission of the Joyce Ketay Agency, 630 9th Ave., Suite 706, New York, NY 10036. All rights reserved. The entire text of *Jar the Floor* has been published in an acting edition by Dramatists Play Service, 440 Park Ave. S., New York, NY 10016, 212-MU3-8960 (ph), 212-213-1539 (fx).

THE LAST CARBURETOR by Leon Chase Copyright 2002 by Leon Chase. Reprinted by permission of the author. All rights reserved. The entire text of *The Last Carburetor* has been published by NY Theatre Experience in *Plays and Playwrights 2003*

LIMONADE TOUS LES JOURS by Charles L. Mee Copyright 2001 by Charles L. Mee. Reprinted by permission of International Creative Management (Attn.: Libby Edwards, assistant to Martin Kooij), 40 W. 57th St., New York, NY 10019. All rights reserved. The entire text of *Limonade Tous Les Jours* has been published by Smith and Kraus, Inc. in *Humana Festival 2002: The Complete Plays*